The Ernst & Young Information Management Series

Managing Information Strategically

Also from Ernst & Young

The Ernst & Young Guide to Total Cost Management
The Complete Guide to Special Event Management
The Ernst & Young Guide to Raising Capital
The Ernst & Young Guide to Expanding in the Global Market
Understanding and Using Financial Data: An Ernst & Young
    Guide for Attorneys
The Ernst & Young Business Plan Guide, Second Edition

Forthcoming from Ernst & Young

(Titles subject to change)

Mergers & Acquisitions, Second Edition
Development Effectiveness: Creating High Performance
    Information Services Organizations in the 1990s
    (The Ernst & Young Information Management Series)
Information Technology and Banking: The Restructuring of an
    Industry (The Ernst & Young Information Management
    Series)
The Ernst & Young Almanac of Best U.S. Business Cities
The Name of the Game is Money: The Business of Sports
Privatization: Investing in Infrastructure

The Ernst & Young Information Management Series

Managing Information Strategically

**By James V. McGee and
Laurence Prusak,
The Ernst & Young Center for
Information Technology and Strategy
with Philip J. Pyburn**

John Wiley & Sons, Inc.
New York • Brisbane • Chichester • Singapore • Toronto

Library of Congress Cataloging in Publication Data

Managing information strategically / Ernst & Young.
    p.   cm. — (The Ernst & Young information management series)
    Includes bibliographical references.
    ISBN 0-471-57544-5
    1. Management information systems. 2. Information resources
management. 3. Strategic planning. I. Ernst & Young. II. Series.
HD30.2.E76   1993
658.4′038—dc20   92-37939
                                        CIP

Printed in the United States of America

10 9 8 7 6 5

To our families: full of both information and strategies

Contents

Preface

Why another book on information and strategy?

The promise of information technology has been clear from the very beginning. High-speed digital computers would make it possible for organizations to excel by delivering "the right information, at the right time, to the right place." But accomplishing this goal has proven significantly harder than expected.

The limits of technology or the lack of implementation skills are the usual suspects, when this promise fails to materialize. Managers continue to believe that the next generation of technology will bring the "silver bullet" that will finally solve the vexing information problem. Or that better technical experts will create the missing link between business opportunity and technology promise. But organizations today that target suspects like these are deceiving themselves.

We have no doubts that information-technology products and services will continue to evolve at a dizzying rate, offering solutions to old problems and opening up new opportunities. But "technology limits" are no longer viable excuses for ongoing failures in applying information technology to meet organizational needs.

"Implementation limits" offer no better excuse. We can recite our share of implementation horror stories. On a case-by-case basis, there will always be organizations that fail to implement particular technology dreams. But this is no more true of information technology than any other strategic resource. Although implementing complex systems is hard, it can be done. For every horror story, there is a success story. The knowledge and the skills exist to implement any given system, if the need is clear enough.

The fundamental problem still remains: to define "the *right* information, the *right* time, and the *right* place."

This is a definition that can be provided only by those executives charged with making consequential decisions for organizations. The answer, "all the information, right away, and everywhere," is untenable, no matter how often it is the implicit message in technology sales pitches or lazy information plans.

This book represents our effort to help executives work through their own answers to the linkage of information and strategy. It does not devote much attention to the specific limits of today's technology or the likely developments of tomorrow's.

As is clear, the answers don't reside in technology. Over the first several decades of computer use in organizations, people interpreted the accidental technology limits of the day as defining the "natural and inevitable" future of computer application in organizations. The technology of large, expensive mainframes implied the inevitable centralization of organizational structure and management authority. The arrival of minicomputers and improved telecommunications technologies justified the "rightness" of distributed and decentralized computing. And the later arrival of personal computers brought its own rhetoric about "power to the people," and the "PC as the great equalizer." Organizations disappeared as individuals became electronic entrepreneurs, selling services to the highest bidder.

All of these technological choices are possible, feasible, and economical. Technology doesn't impose limits on organizations; it opens up alternatives. The challenge becomes to choose usefully (as opposed to "correctly") among them. Such choices do not generally require intimate knowledge of internal technical detail, anymore than consumers' choices among automobiles require knowledge of internal combustion engines.

Realizing the full strategic potential of information is more about thinking than doing. We've heard that IBM has replaced its traditional slogan, "Think," with "Do." This may prove to be an unfortunate choice.

The person we have kept in mind as this book's reader is the manager or executive who Donald Schon of MIT describes as, the "reflective practitioner." These are individuals whose slogan is "think then do," individuals held accountable for timely actions who can balance possibilities against practical constraints to find the innovative solution.

"Innovation," unfortunately, cannot be reduced to checklists or well-specified procedures. Our charter at the Center for Information Technology and Strategy is to look beyond the boundaries of current practice. We try to work as advance scouts, probing a few steps ahead along promising paths. Some steps may prove to be wrong turns or lead to dead ends. The organizations that want to achieve strategic success can't wait until all the answers are known.

Therefore, this book is not as much a guide or "how to" about managing information as it is a guide about how to think of the problem; how to weigh possible responses in light of technology, organizational culture, and corporate finance; and finally, how to remain sensitive to the needs of a dynamic information strategy.

The obvious applications of information technology have been implemented. Strategic success with information depends on inventing nonobvious applications. This requires some sense of the state of the technologically possible. More importantly, it requires a deep appreciation for strategy, viewed from an information centered perspective.

We have found it useful to think of strategy as a three-part problem. First, there is the challenge of designing an artful plan for achieving distinction in the marketplace. Then, there is the challenge of marshaling and deploying the necessary resources to execute that plan. Finally, there is the challenge of integrating design with execution, as the plan unfolds in the competitive environment. Design, execution, and integration must all come together to realize an organization's full strategic potential.

We attempt to advance the thinking about the role information can play in each of these three parts. For strategy design, what does it mean to treat information as a resource that's every bit as important as labor or capital? As a strategic resource, information needs to be managed on a daily basis with the same care and attention given the organization's human and financial resources. To do so, organizations must invest in well-structured processes for managing information. Structurally, these processes should support and reinforce one another, creating an information space within which individuals can carry out their daily tasks. These information management processes and information architecture should be designed and developed with a full appreciation for the political dimensions of information. For strategy execution to function smoothly, information process and architecture should encourage desired information behaviors and discourage undesired behaviors.

Finally, information provides the central nervous system that integrates strategy and action. At one level, information drives the feedback loops that ensure that execution is aligned with design. At a second level, information drives the feedback loops that drive organizational learning, ensuring that strategy design can adapt to a dynamic competitive environment.

Acknowledgments

We would like to thank Bud Mathaisel, the Director of Ernst & Young's Center for Information Technology and Strategy, for his ongoing support for this project, his feedback, and his care. Alan Stanford, Ernst & Young's National Director of IT Consulting, had the original idea for the Center and did the work to see it up and running. The Center is an unusual organizational learning effort in its own right and has demanded its share of vision and commitment from the senior levels of Ernst & Young's management. This volume is one of the results of that vision.

Many of the ideas presented here have developed and evolved in conversations and joint projects with our colleages at the Center. In particular, we would like to thank Tom Davenport, Vaughn Merlyn, and Mary Silva Doctor for their input and contributions. Jennifer Burgin, Todd Bricker, Carol Hladick, Susan Sutherland, Tia DeWeese, and Janet Santry provided critical support conducting background research, preparing graphics, and word processing.

Professor Robert Eccles of the Harvard Business School

has worked closely with us on a variety of projects over the past several years. Some of the results of that work have found their way into this work. We gratefully acknowledge his assistance.

Jon Zonderman, our editor, played a significant role helping us to clarify and articulate our thoughts. Other friends and colleagues who have contributed to his effort in varied ways include: Mark Hauser, Steve Levine, Mike Ashmore, Mike Gauthier, Benn Konsynski, Dorothy Leonard–Barton, John Henderson, and Jim Cash. We're quite sure we've forgotten someone but beg their forgiveness and understanding.

As our dedication suggests, our families have helped and supported us in ways "measureless to man." Spouses and children always bear the costs but rarely share in any of the tangible benefits. A thank-you in the Acknowledgments seems small recompense.

Figure 1-1 is reprinted with the permission of The Free Press, a division of Macmillan, Inc. from *Competitive Strategy: Techniques for Analyzing Industries and Competitors* by Michael E. Porter. Copyright © 1980 by The Free Press.

Figure 1-4 is reprinted with the permission of The Free Press, a division of Macmillan, Inc. from *Competitive Advantage: Creating and Sustaining Superior Performance* by Michael E. Porter. Copyright © 1985 by Michael E. Porter.

Figure 2-3 is reprinted by permission of *Harvard Business Review*. An exhibit from "The Core Competence of the Corporation," by C.K. Prahalad and G. Hamel, 68(3). Copyright © 1990 by the President and Fellows of Harvard College; all rights reserved.

PART I

Introduction

Introduction

Over the last 25 years the industrialized world has been making the transition from an industrial economy to an information economy, and for the next several decades, information—rather than land or capital—will drive the creation of wealth and prosperity. In this kind of economy, it is what you know, not what you own, that determines success. During the 1970s and 1980s, General Motors learned that controlling the capital base of the largest industrial corporation in the world provided little advantage in the face of organizations that were better informed about shifting customers' demands, better informed about how to organize manufacturing processes to serve these demands, and more willing to act on the basis of such information. Whatever competitive advantage might have accrued to economies of scale could be offset by effective deployment and use of information.

In an information economy, organizations compete on the basis of their ability to acquire, manipulate, interpret, and use information effectively. Organizations that master this information competition will be the big winners in the future, while

1

organizations that don't will be quickly overtaken by their rivals.

As the General Motors example suggests, information-enabled competition is not synonymous with investments in information technology. Organizations have certainly invested vast sums in the application of computer and communication technologies to their problems. That does not make them information-enabled competitors. The strategic success of American Airlines, Federal Express, Wal-Mart, Frito-Lay, and others can be credited, in part, to shrewd use of information and effective exploitation of the possibilities inherent in information technology. While not necessarily leveraged with information technology, the R&D prowess of Merck and the real estate management skills of McDonald's are clearly information intensive aspects of their strategic success.

Other examples of information and information technology use are more problematic. The introduction of automatic teller machines has certainly made life more convenient for thousands of consumers. Whether the banks who first invested in this technology made permanent gains in market share, or simply raised the stakes for all competitors, without having altered competitive positioning, is by no means clear.

At the macroeconomic level, the business benefits of investments in information processing technology are far from clear. Stephen Roach, chief economist at Morgan Stanley, and Gary Loveman, from the Harvard Business School, have argued that investments in information technology have led to little or no measurable increases in aggregate white-collar productivity in the U.S. Although few organizations would be willing to operate without these technologies, no one has managed, as yet, to refute these charges in any systematic way.

There is a way to sort through the confusion surrounding the relationship between information technology and both competition and productivity. Information technology investments create no more advantage or productivity, by themselves, than do investments in new machine tools. It is not technology but technology-in-use that creates value. The value of information technology depends on information and the role of information in organizations. Information can create significant value for organizations by enabling new products and services and by improving the quality of decision making throughout the organization. This is not, however, a necessary outcome.

The creation, capture, organization, distribution, interpretation, and commercialization of information are key information processes. The technology used to enable these information processes is considerably less important than the information that systems hold. *Information* is dynamic, capable of creating great value, and is the glue that holds enterprises together. *Information Technology* can be an important enabler of better information use, but it can just as easily be "dead metal"—useless without information and human users.

The Information Technology Age

Information technology has irreversibly changed the business world. The ways organizations perform their operations, design their products, and market their products have all changed dramatically since the serious introduction of information technology in the mid-1950s. More and more often, products themselves are built around the capabilities of information technology—from remote controls for VCRs to the antilock braking systems in automobiles. This revolution has not been cheap. Since World War II, trillions of dollars have been invested in information technology. Whole new industries, such as the computer industry, have sprung up which contain some of the largest enterprises on earth.

Beyond the business world, information technology has changed the forms, processes, and often, the substance of how we live our lives. In the developed world children learn the principles of computing at an early age—their toys are often based on technology. Individuals interact every day with dozens of devices that contain some form of computer. Computer technology may be as obvious as the notebook computer in an executive's briefcase or as subtle as the chip that controls the sprinkler system which waters the front lawn.

The economics of advancing information technology is creating an environment of "ubiquitous computing" that is today transforming the business environment and will ultimately transform much of the social and home environment as well. Information technology is quickly making the boundary between work and home fuzzier then it has ever been.

Unmet Promises

The contrast between the massive investments in information technology, its clear transforming potential, and the equivocal gains actually realized has contributed to a growing sense among organizations that they must reexamine many of their most fundamental assumptions about how they structure and conduct their use of information and information technology. Information technology investments were touted by vendors, consultants, and journalists as tools that would create a "white-collar revolution." Information technology would enable a paperless office where all employees—executive and clerk alike—would be "empowered" to make more creative and significant contributions to a firm's mission.

It is sad to say, but little of this has come to pass. Stephen Roach's research suggests that white-collar productivity hasn't improved much at all in the past twenty years despite the magnitude of investment. As far as the paperless office goes, anyone working in an office knows the truth about this oft-maligned concept. Businesses spend over $125 billion for paper each year and the firms that make traditional file cabinets are still doing well.

Another siren call that has drawn many proponents in the past two decades is the concept that investments in information technology can be strategic—that they can create sustainable competitive advantage. This idea gained momentum when it appeared that firms like American Airlines, with its Sabre reservation system, and American Hospital Supply, with its order entry system, had done just this—consciously invested time, money, and senior management focus to build an information system that paid tremendous strategic dividends and would continue to have such a payback well into the future.

Time and greater perspective suggest that these systems are less the product of a conscious strategic act and more a response to internal needs.[1] And while there are obvious short-term business advantages to being first with a new system, the market ensures that such advantages will continue to be short-term.

Where's the Value?

All revolutions generate rhetoric. Vendors hope to create market awareness for their products. Consultants, academics, and industry journalists all need to feed their respective distribution channels with news or ideas. The capabilities of information technologies can be mind-boggling, even, or perhaps especially, for those with expert knowledge. The capabilities offer the promise of solving difficult organizational problems.

There are cultural foundations that exacerbate these attitudes and they are particularly American. The idea that complex problems and situations can be readily "fixed" by the alliance of money and machines is powerful and alluring. While there are occasions and situations where this is true, it is certainly not a model to be universally adopted. The idea has caused firms to expend billions of dollars chasing an elusive and ultimately false goal.

Where, then, is the value in information technology systems as we enter the twenty-first century? It is our thesis that *information* itself provides the greatest potential payback to organizations. Stated simply, this may seem self-evidently true and not worthy of further discussion. Yet the dizzying pace of change in information technology industries tends to keep attention focused more on what the technology can do and less on why these new capabilities matter. Shifting the focus to wrestling with information questions before turning to the technology can yield great benefits in understanding the strategic dimension of information.

Take, for example, a well-known fast-food chain. It is widely understood within the company that the selection and acquisition of restaurant sites is absolutely central to competitive success. The company's strategy statements and plans are full of references to such questions as how to find the optimal restaurant locations, how those locations will be acquired, which restaurants should be owned versus leased, and so on. They even identify the "core competencies"[2] of site selection and negotiation as critical to the company's long-term success.

What these statements do not have, however, is an explicit recognition of the information that is needed to locate stores effectively. Stated from an information perspective, the company would describe its core competencies along the following lines: "we must have the best information about possible sites, the most detailed insight into demographic and community growth patterns, and the most sophisticated analytic techniques for evaluating possible sites. And, because we compete on a global basis, this information must be global." While this may not sound very different from saying that site selection is critical to the company's success, it makes an enormous difference in the way the company implements its strategy.

The implication of this explicit recognition that location information is central to the company's success would lead it to develop formal mechanisms to acquire, manipulate, and use that information. Think of the strategic advantage that any company would have had if it had had the data, and the analytical tools with which to transform the data into information, with regard to Disney's land acquisition in central Florida 30 years ago! Individual speculators made informed bets, and some made fortunes, working with what little information they may have acquired haphazardly. How much more might have been possible by implementing systematic processes and technology for acquiring and analyzing potentially relevant real estate information?

How This Book is Organized

Competing strategically can be treated as a three-part problem. Companies must design strategies, translate these designs into daily action, and ensure an effective ongoing integration of the design and the action. This three-part activity takes place within a competitive environment replete with information of actual and potential relevance. Figure I-1 is a schematic representation of these relationships. This book's discussion of the role of information and strategy parallels this three-part structure. Chapter One considers the entire competitive strategy problem from the perspective of information. It is helpful to look at some of the old chestnuts from the "competitive uses of IT" tradition from the perspective of information rather than information technology. In each case, the technology, while necessary, was tangential to the real breakthroughs that the company made. The strategic advantage came as the result of the effective management and organizational use of the information that was being managed by the technology.

In fact, because the technology was available to all competitors, the benefits realized by companies from any given technology innovation could quickly be duplicated by the en-

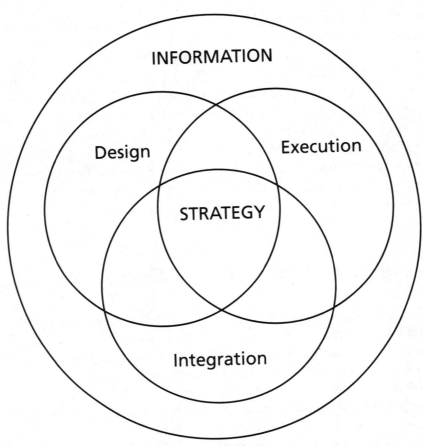

Figure I.1   *Information and Competitive Strategy*

tire industry. But a truly world-class information capability, such as American Airlines' knowledge of passenger traffic, loading factors, and so on, provides an edge that is substantially more difficult to duplicate. It is more difficult to duplicate because the advantage is built into the operational and management processes of the organization, which are significantly harder to understand and replicate than the more visible elements of technology that support the processes. For the most successful users of information, continuing improvements in information management make it nearly impossible for rivals to catch up. Sophistication in managing and exploiting information creates a positive feedback loop; information begets information and knowledge begets knowledge.

Part I of the book examines the role of information in the strategy design process itself. As a routine management process, strategic planning is highly information-intensive, and would benefit from focusing more explicit attention on information management within the process. More importantly, however, strategy design choices change when information is treated as a resource equal in status and stature to other conventional strategic resources of capital, labor, and technology. Chapter Two reviews how information can leverage traditional strategy design choices and create opportunities for new strategies. Strategy design attempts to identify how a company can differentiate itself from competitors in terms of product/service design or create sustainable economic advantages of scale or scope. These design choices include decisions about the positioning and scope of products and services, the development and maintenance of core competences for delivering products and services, and the selection of organizational structures and processes to integrate the company into a functioning whole that is itself integrated into the competitive environment. Information introduces new degrees of freedom and opportunities for leverage for each of these design dimensions.

Chapter Three explores the implications of competing and cooperating in a world of electronic commerce. Possibly the most critical influence of information on strategy design is the increasing trend toward greater electronic interaction between organizations. In more organizations and industries, the data used for conducting day-to-day business operations with suppliers and customers is transmitted *between* organizations in machine-readable form. The implementation of electronic data interchange (EDI) to support the exchange of order and invoicing information, the exchange of computer-aided design (CAD) data between contractors and subcontractors during the design of new products, and the exchange of electronic mail between knowledge workers in separate organizations are all early examples of a general business environment in which all routine business will be conducted electronically. Within the next several years, electronic commerce will be as commonplace and standard as doing business by telephone is today. Also in this chapter, we consider how organizations implementing these early prototypes of an electronic business environment will need to manage their relations with customers and suppliers on a more cooperative basis. This cooperative business environment is culturally embedded in the industrial systems of Japan and Western Europe. How can we use the emerging technological infrastructure to effectively balance cooperative behavior and the pursuit of competitive advantage?

Part II looks more in-depth at how the management of information within organizations affects the execution of the strategies they design. Information, and information technology in particular, has always played an important role in the day-to-day activities of companies. We have a good understanding of how to use information and information technology within routine processes such as manufacturing, sales, marketing, and other execution activities. But little attention has been given to finding ways to effectively capitalize on information from an integrative perspective.

If information is fundamental to competitive strategy, how should organizations manage such a critical resource? Despite the vast quantities of data managed by computer-based systems, many thoughtful analysts estimate that machine-readable data constitutes less than 10% of the information resources within an average organization. Much more data resides in paper files and other locations outside the bounds of current computer-based systems. Still more information lies in the heads of the skilled members of the organization. How can organizations do a more effective job in identifying their "information situation"? What policies and processes will lead to increased value for these "invisible information assets" without creating new bureaucracies of technical information specialists? How can we best meet the information needs of all levels of the organization—production workers through senior executives—not just the more easily identified needs of accountants and financial analysts? How can we integrate the growing volumes of internally generated information with the even faster growing volumes of externally generated information relevant to the organization? Chapters Four and Five address these questions in the context of creating a comprehensive information management process and information architecture for the organization.

"Process" and architecture should be mutually reinforcing dimensions of information management. "Process" focuses on the dynamic aspects of managing information. What should organizations do to be more explicit and systematic in the ways they identify, acquire, evaluate, analyze, package, and disseminate information? What are the appropriate steps and sequence of steps that lead to effective information use in decision making? "Information architecture" focuses on effectively defining and establishing the information space within which information management processes operate. Chapter Five develops the metaphor of architecture as it is applied to information; it identifies both the benefits of such a perspective and critical limits of the analogy.

Even from a strategic perspective, identifying and explicitly managing a much higher percentage of an organization's information resources is only half the equation. Chapter Six turns to the other half of the equation by looking at the human dimensions of information behavior and politics. We need to improve both the individual's ability to make use of information and the organization's ability to make better use of information-leveraged individuals. If you accept the arguments about information and strategy, then "information is power" becomes more relevant than ever. Understanding the "politics of information" is an important factor in how information is used, exchanged, and valued within the organization. People barter for information, use it to wield power over others, or exchange it for other information that they feel will have greater value. The same political factors that influence strategy and capital allocation decisions influence information. "Information in organizations is not innocent."[3] Managing information strategically also implies managing it shrewdly. As such, information management is a part of the executive agenda, something which cannot simply be delegated to technical specialists. Many failures of information technology have been failures to attend to these political dimensions.

Part III, the final part of the book, turns to the central role of information in integrating strategy design and execution. Integration is treated last because companies must first understand the design and execution dimensions, before the possibilities of using information to improve organizational integration will become evident.

Chapter Seven considers how internal information systems that would support executive and management processes might evolve. In these processes, perhaps more than anywhere else, it becomes critical to keep clear the distinctions between information and information technology. Confusing the technology with the information has generated many technical solutions to non-existent problems, and has created new information problems, rather than eliminating them. The lure of technology is understandable. What is more managerial than using information to make decisions? What is more desirable than to have access to *the* information more quickly and in more detail? What does technology do better than move and manipulate masses of information? Certainly vendors of executive information and decision support tools promise, and frequently provide, powerful access to the machine-readable data available in the organization. All too often, however, these technology-driven solutions merely contribute to information overload instead of better-informed management decisions. Arguably, these solutions can even undermine management's confidence in its decision-making capabilities by contributing to a sense of "analysis paralysis"—the hope that the golden nugget of information is out there somewhere, and that the next query or report will yield *the* answer.

There are two converging trends to evaluate from an information-centric perspective. First, leading organizations in a range of industries have begun rethinking how they measure performance against their strategic objectives. They are working diligently to define multiple measures of performance—both financial and non-financial—that would provide earlier feedback on the success or failure of strategy. Second, technology vendors are offering a wider and richer array of tools to support the data analysis and reporting desires of executives. With far more raw data that can be captured electronically, organizations must explicitly work through the data that is presented to executives as most useful. Now that organizations are less constrained (if at all) by technical feasibility, how should executive information systems be designed and implemented? How does an information-centric point of view lead to different recommendations about these particular internal systems' applications?

Chapter Eight concludes the argument by addressing the contributions that information has made to organizational learning. Learning has become a popular goal in recent years. It is certainly difficult to conceive actively promoting "not learning." Learning is the underlying engine that keeps strategy design and execution synchronized in a competitive environment whose predominant feature is change. Valid and timely information is one of the key resources needed to fuel learning in organizations. Information and information technology can play a much more effective role in supporting organizational learning when that role is thought through explicitly. In fact, learning becomes the central process by which to translate into effective action new thinking about the role of information in competitive strategy.

The strategic message posed by an information economy is clear:

- Information is increasingly becoming the basis of competition.

- Information management needs should drive technology alternatives.

Therefore,

- Executives must explicitly identify the role that information will play in their company's competitive strategy.

Notes

1. Hopper, M. D. (1990). "Rattling SABRE—New Ways to Compete on Information." *Harvard Business Review* **68**(3):118–125.

2. March, J. G. (1988). *Decisions and Organizations.* Cambridge, MA, Basil Blackwell.

3. Prahalad, C. K. and G. Hamel (1990) "The Core Competence of the Corporation." *Harvard Business Review* **68**(3):79–91.

Information and Competition

The emergence of an information or knowledge-based economy has already achieved the status of cliché. Nonetheless, few organizations or executives have demonstrated that they have integrated this knowledge into their strategies in any substantive way. There are two possible explanations for this discrepancy. First, while talking about the information age may make for innocuous after-dinner speeches, it does not effect any significant change to mainstream business practice. Or second, taking advantage of the strategic possibilities of improved information is substantially harder than it looks.

For executives who find the second explanation more likely, the strategic problem posed by the information economy can be stated in the following way:

■ Information will increasingly form the basis of competition, especially in the service sector, but also in manufacturing.

■ Senior executives must begin to *explicitly* articulate and define the role information will play in the design and execution of their company's competitive strategy, or they will risk being at a serious disadvantage to the hands of information-enabled rivals.

For most organizations, investments in the tools for managing information (chiefly computers and telecommunications networks) have become a significant component of capital investment budgets. In financial services industries, information technology budgets *are* the capital budgets. At that level, information has become a strategic issue. Deriving value from these investments by deriving greater value from the data they manage and manipulate has not received the same level of attention.

Where there has been a focus on extracting strategic value from information investments, it has been on the masses of quantitative and transaction-oriented data maintained by large information processing systems. Far less attention has been devoted to deriving strategic value from doing a better job managing other forms of critical information; information that is more qualitative and diffused throughout the organization.

Information appears as a topic of discussion in almost all aspects of organization and strategy. Thinking about strategy breaks down into a three-part problem. First, there is a design problem of identifying and crafting a match between marketplace opportunities and organizational capabilities. Early research on strategic planning focused on planning processes for managing the design effort. More recent research has turned to developing better grounded theories of the economic drivers of particular strategy alternatives.

The second part of the strategy problem is to ensure that the organization has the skills and capabilities to understand and execute the designed strategy. Strategies can fail either at the design or the execution stage. The total quality movement and the recent attention on business process innovation represent efforts to improve the ability of organizations to execute their strategies effectively.

The final dimension of the strategy problem is to effectively integrate design with execution. The volatility and unpredictability of the economic environment in the past few years clearly demonstrate that no strategy lasts forever. There is no hope of articulating a single strategy design that will withstand all challenges. Consequently, organizations must create measurement and feedback systems that will improve the flow of information between strategy design and execution so that they can learn from and act on the results of their execution efforts when designing new strategies.

Throughout this three-part problem, information plays an essential role. In the next sections of this chapter, the contribution of information to each dimension of strategy is reviewed. Some of the more widely known examples of information-enabled strategies are revisited within this organizing framework to discover whether new lessons can be gleaned from familiar stories. In subsequent chapters, each of these broad topics—design, execution, and integration—is developed from an information-centric point of view.

Information and Competition: A Framework for Analysis

Two terms need to be defined to set up the discussion that follows—strategy and information. Both seem to be precise, and yet are used by individuals to talk about wildly disparate concepts. The definitions here are mainstream and risk repeating the obvious to ensure that the discussion begins from a common starting point.

Strategy

While the acquisition and use of capital remain factors in competitive strategy, they no longer form the basis of real comparative advantage. By the end of the 1980s it was apparent that no firm was too big to be acquired nor dominant to the extent that it was not subject to shifting patterns of competition (witness RJR Nabisco and IBM). Companies that focus on absolute size, and the economies of scale or scope that place size as the centerpiece of their strategy, assume the greatest risk from their information-enabled rivals. The historic advantages accrued by those companies with the largest investments in plant, equipment, and distribution capabilities no longer exist. Like the Maginot Line, they represent the barriers of a bygone era; an era in which size ensured market dominance, and precluded most competition.

The shifting basis of competitive advantage is a natural by-product of the shift from the industrial economy, where the effective deployment of capital was the key to success, to the information economy, where information is the key. Yet few executives have shifted their thinking to focus directly on the information they must dominate to compete in the 21st century.

Thinking about the nature of competitive strategy and effective roles for information and information technology is evolving rapidly. Scholars, consultants, and executives all wrestle with the most effective ways to think about strategy problems. On one side, the global economic and competitive environment is increasing the need for a deeper understanding of strategy. Organizations must cope with more competitors pursuing more diverse strategies than they ever had to in simply domestic markets. Customer diversity and diversity in regulatory and economic environments also adds to the problem of strategic complexity.

On the other side, a richer understanding of information and the potentials of developing technologies increases the possible degrees of freedom in crafting organizations that can survive and flourish in this environment. What are the strategic consequences of allowing design engineers at Northrup to communicate directly and electronically with their subcontracted counterparts while designing the B-2 bomber? For most organizations, the questions were difficult to ask. Developing answers will take longer still.

A company's competitive strategy defines its businesses, how it will operate those businesses, and particularly, how it will differentiate its products and services from those of the competition. Thus, a comprehensive strategy must address two sets of issues, as well as their integration. First, strategies must articulate the company's customers and market segments that the organization wishes to serve. Second, strategies must articulate the skills and resources that the organization must marshal to provide products and services to these markets. Both issues critically depend on information. Defining potential customers and markets depends on external information about needs and artful interpretation of these needs in terms that can tap the strengths of the organization.

Translating choices about customers and markets into the

internal components of strategy must consider the following issues at a minimum:

1. The definition and design of the **products and services** that will be offered.

2. The setting of **performance objectives**—both financial and non-financial—for the organization.

3. The design of **organizational and operational processes** that will meet the performance objectives by **differentiating** the company's products and services from those of competitors.

4. The **deployment of resources** in such a way that the performance objectives will most likely be achieved.

5. The **monitoring** of organizational performance and the redirection of resources as required.

The most current thinking about how to articulate answers to these issues has been in terms of the notion of core competences.[1] This is an update and extension of classic strategic planning advice: to inventory corporate strengths and weaknesses. The notion of core competence articulates these internal capabilities in terms that can be better applied to strategy design. The simplest example of core competence is Sony's ability to miniaturize electronic products. This particular competence is composed of a variety of specialized skills and knowledge that, once identified, can be directed toward new strategy opportunities.

The issue of differentiation is fundamental to an understanding of competitive strategy, because an effective strategy must define the ways that a company's products and services will be superior to those of its rivals (and potential rivals) *in the eyes of its customers*. If a strategy does not allow a company to offer (or at least convince customers that it offers) higher quality, lower cost, better service, or some other desirable characteristic, then there is no strategy. Without this ability to clearly differentiate products and services from those of the competition, a company cannot hope to achieve superior performance.

Of course, just setting strategic objectives is not enough—there must be a practical way to achieve those objectives, leveraging the talents and skills of the company's employees. Therefore, one way to think about competitive strategy is as a logical and consistent "story" that motivates employees to achieve the company's objectives. In this sense, a strategy defines the organization's place in the competitive environment and the way it will improve that position relative to significant rivals. It defines the products and services employees will develop and sell, and how these products will satisfy customer needs. And perhaps most importantly, it establishes a performance benchmark against which employees can adapt and learn from the results of their actions.

Information

Although information is an asset that needs to be managed, like human, capital, land, and physical assets, in practice, it is a class apart from other assets. These differences define the promise of information as well as the challenges of managing information. Information is infinitely reusable, it doesn't deteriorate or depreciate, and its value is determined solely by its user; one person's gold is another's dross.

While managing information is as important as managing other assets, knowledge about information management is not as systematically developed or codified. Although there is much knowledge and research about information, its characteristics, and alternatives for managing it, this knowledge tends to be fragmented, misunderstood, and misapplied.

Knowledge about finance and operations management has been collected and taught for more than a century. Knowledge about how to manage information has been collected only recently; in fact, the kinds of unifying definitions of information and information management that allow for the collection and dissemination of this knowledge are only now appearing.

Before we can discuss how to manage information, we need to fully understand what information is. Some argue that information is simply a collection of data, that if you take a stream of financial data and put it on a page, you have given a person information. As with many new concepts, organizations are initially working to manage information by way of analogy with better known fields. Thus, information is described by way of analogy as an asset or a flow, a first step toward improving information management. These analogies suggest possible concepts or tools for managing information that can be borrowed from other fields.

Information is not just data collected; rather, it is data collected, organized, ordered, and imbued with meaning and context. Information must *inform*, while data has no such mandate. Information must be *bounded*, while data can be limitless. In order for data to become *useful* to a decision maker as information, it must be presented in such a way that he or she can relate to it and act upon it.

To a degree, information is in the eye of the beholder. Although seemingly trite, this observation makes a different point. Data can be considered and discussed in isolation. Information must be discussed in the context of specific users and decision makers. Information is data in use, and use implies a user.

Maybe early attempts to create management information systems failed because the attempts organized data into forms that were meaningful to computer programmers and data organizers, but didn't enable managers to pose questions regarding the data, to relate to it, or to manipulate the data to acquire information.

In short, individuals are never really given information. They create information from their own reading, relation to, and context for data; or, they receive a presentation in the form of a book, memo, report, CD-ROM, or other medium, which someone else's reading has provided; or, more often, individuals listen or talk to other individuals who have read (or heard), related to, and provided context for data.

Before falling into infinite regress, suffice it to say that we are surrounded by data, and organizations are abuzz with data that may turn out to be valuable information to some user with a decision problem. Consider the varieties of data encountered by just a handful of individuals over the course of a few days. I read of a competitor's plans for a new factory in a trade journal. You hear an interesting anecdote on a radio talk show. Your boss meets with the executive vice president to discuss next year's budget. In the evening, my spouse offers a tidbit gleaned from a professional journal, yours tells of a seminar in a related field. Over drinks, we overhear a rumor of impending legislation on tax reform. By week's end we are awash in data.

But what do we do with it? How do we organize it? And how does the 3,000-employee "knowledge worker" company that we all work for siphon and package the information in such a way that a colleague in Chicago, Tokyo, or Sydney could present it next week?

One of the Bell operating companies, despite the state-of-the-art technology in much of the network, maintains a number of large mechanical switches in rural parts of its region. While the technology is being phased out—to be replaced within the next decade—the workers who know how to repair these switches are retiring and will likely be gone before the last switch is replaced.

Several years ago, management began to worry; how could they get people to learn how to repair these switches? They never thought to ask the aging repair technicians. They considered contracting with a consulting firm for advice, or building an expert system to capture repair information that younger workers could tap.

While management was worrying, the older repair technicians and some of the newer technicians were doing what colleagues around the world do: going out together after work for a drink, or a bite to eat, talking over lunch, hanging out together at company picnics, etc. What was happening? The older technicians were teaching the younger workers how to maintain the ancient switches.

When management announced a special training session on repairing the old switches, the younger staff said, "they didn't need to attend; they had already learned the techniques during after-work gatherings."

This is the kind of information management practiced in most organizations. It's a wonderful story—full of teamwork, pride in one's craft, and camaraderie. What it doesn't show, however, is the kind of systematic management of information companies will need if they hope to outlive those mechanical switches.

Design and Execution

Competitive strategy is both a design and execution problem. Clever and insightful competitive strategy design, whether it be repositioning a fading brand to appeal to a newly defined market niche, or uniquely combining technologies to create a new product category, is only an armchair exercise until it is translated into day-to-day activities in the marketplace. While early attention in understanding strategy focused on improving the design process, recent attention has shifted to the equal challenges of execution.

Information and information technology have always had roles in both strategy design and execution. They have a role to play in improving the design of competitive strategies, the ability to execute these strategies, and the ability to ensure that strategies and execution remain synchronized with one another and with the competitive environment. As the *integration* of strategy and execution becomes the central organizational challenge, the role of information as a key tool for achieving this integration becomes clearer. Focusing on information allows companies to address how they will deliver superior performance, and turn strategy into something concrete and actionable. This design, execution, and integration structure for thinking about strategy offers three perspectives to examine relative to information:

- **Information and Strategy Design.** Information about the competitive environment and the current organization helps executives identify both threats to and opportunities for the company, and sets the stage for the design of a more effective competitive response. Information also functions as a critical resource for the design of strategy alternatives.

- **Information and Strategy Execution.** Information technology enables new alternatives for designing processes that create and deliver products and services. Information represents one of the most important and malleable features executives can use to differentiate products and services. In some cases, information is even the product itself.

- **Information and Integration.** The feedback of performance information is central to the creation of an adaptive "learning" organization, which at once executes the strategic achievement of its objectives and recognizes the need to modify those objectives when they become ineffective.

Information and Strategy Design

Professor Michael Porter at the Harvard Business School has developed the most commonly accepted framework for organizing the design of competitive strategy. It has withstood sustained testing in the marketplace and has emerged as a common organizing framework for evaluating strategy design alternatives. He suggests that effective strategy must take into account not only the actions and reactions of direct rivals, but also the roles of suppliers and customers, and alternative products that satisfy the same basic need and the prospect that new entrants (perhaps with different capabilities) will enter the fray (Figure 1-1). Porter points out that the power of suppliers and customers relative to the company and its competitors, the barriers to entry that are likely to limit new competition, and the availability of alternative products that perform essentially the same function, all influence the nature of competition (and thus the attractiveness) of an industry.

The power of the Porter Model from an information perspective is that it encourages executives to explicitly consider a broader range of strategic information than is typical in most companies. Traditionally, executives have thought about "the

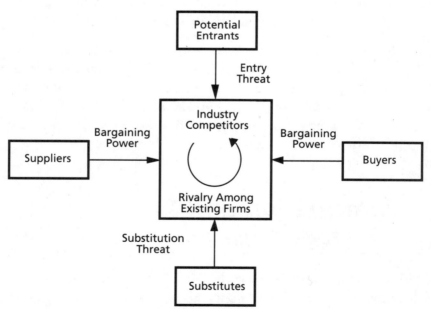

Figure 1.1   *Porter Model of Competitive Forces*

competition" in terms of rivals within the existing industry—software vendors competing with other software vendors, life insurers competing with other life insurers, and so on. This model suggests that executives must consider alternative products that currently exist and those that might emerge to satisfy customers requirements, and the possibility that new competitors or companies in hitherto unrelated industries might enter the company's markets. In addition, the model adds consideration of important resource suppliers, including "labor," as a factor in the competitive equation. "Competitive information," thus encompasses much more than "information about competitors."

As Figure 1-2 suggests, the model is actually more complicated than it first appears, because each box in Figure 1-1 represents a group of companies operating in their own competitive industry setting. Thus, an aluminum producer sells sheets of can stock to a container manufacturer, who, in turn, is competing with other container manufacturers who sell to

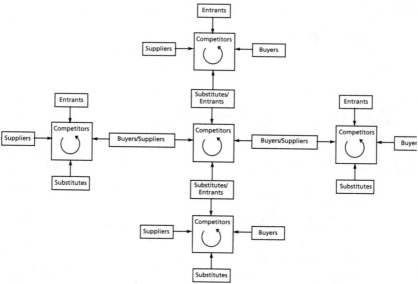

Figure 1.2 *Chains of Industries*

beverage companies, who have their own set of competitive issues and concerns.

Often, the most critical strategic information may exist one or two levels removed from the primary industry under review. For example, the aluminum producer may get more useful insights into future market conditions by understanding the beverage industry than by looking directly at the aluminum industry. How might consumer concerns about the environment influence beverage manufacturers to shift production from aluminum cans to plastic two-liter bottles? Are manufacturers of plastic bottles presenting new threats to the demand for aluminum? Thus, the information base that is necessary to develop effective strategies is becoming larger and more complex.

This information base is also dynamic, because the relationships between many of the industry players are constantly in motion. When the strategist only needed to consider primary rivals, the competitive information base could be updated rather infrequently because these relationships change quite slowly. Now, the strategist must consider hundreds of relationships, some of which change almost daily. Consider how much more difficult the banking strategic planner's information problem becomes when AT&T, Sears, and GM all begin to offer their own credit cards.

Industry Attractiveness

The attractiveness of an industry is based, in large part, on a given company's control relative to the other participants. An attractive industry is one that has significant power to dictate terms and conditions to suppliers and customers, and that encounters little threat of competition from rivals, alternative products, or new entrants. Under such conditions, a company will be able to maintain high prices and negotiate favorable deals with suppliers, maintaining high margins and profitability. When a company has relatively little power compared to its customers and suppliers (caused by facing a surfeit of rivals, having many alternative products, and encountering numerous entry possibilities), margins and profitability will be low.

For example, at one extreme, farming in North America is a decidedly unattractive business because:

- There are thousands of rivals competing for the available customers.

- Since customers (manufacturers, distributors, and grocery chains) are large and powerful, especially relative to the farmer, they can dictate prices paid *to* the farmer.

- Suppliers (of fertilizer, seed, fuels, etc.) are also large relative to the farmer, and they control prices paid *by* the farmer.

- There are a wide range of substitute products that satisfy the consumer's nutritional needs, and consumers can easily make the substitution when price disparities arise (e.g., they will eat rice when corn prices are too high).

- There is a surfeit of arable land in North America (given the information- and technology-enabled levels of productivity possible with today's state-of-the-art), which allows new entrants to emerge quickly when prices are high.

At the other extreme, Xerox competed for many years in a patent-protected environment in which relatively little power rested with customers (if they wanted a copier, Xerox was the only choice), suppliers were relatively small manufacturers of parts and components, and there was no practical substitute for the product, nor the possibility of entry except by another breakthrough invention (which, of course, did not occur). Unsurprisingly, this position attracted many potential competitors, and, the moment Xerox's patents expired, there was a flood of competitive activity, primarily due to the entry of other large, sophisticated companies using variants of the formerly proprietary technology.

The competitive challenge facing a company, then, depends in part on the attractiveness of the industry in which it competes. For a company in a relatively appealing industry, the struggle is to maintain as much of this appeal as possible, while also recognizing that new entrants and new products will emerge in response to the relatively high returns available. For companies in relatively unattractive industries, the challenge is either to find ways to change the power balance, or to move into more attractive industries.

Improving Information Input to the Strategy Design Process

Porter's framework provides a much more analytic and principled basis for the design and evaluation of competitive strategies than do previous models. Consequently, his model increases the demand for information in a variety of forms and from a variety of sources. Competitor analysis requires much more in-depth data about each competitor, as well as data about a larger universe of potential competitors. Potential threats and opportunities initially appear as very weak signals from either the competitive environment or remote areas of the organization.

Information about both the external environment and current and potential competitors is increasingly available, and frequently in machine-readable format. Companies issue annual reports, SEC filings, and press releases. Their executives give speeches and interviews. The business and trade press presents analyses and background stories. Trade associations and government agencies gather and publish statistics. Sales representatives learn about competitor activities as they call on common customers.

The information challenge for strategy design is to ferret out potentially relevant material and make it available for analysis and interpretation. Weak signals need to be detected and amplified. And all of this needs to be done without inundating the planning function with irrelevant or low-value information. Chapter 4 discusses a process approach to managing the acquisition and use of information relevant to the executives and planners in the organization.

Information as a Resource in the Design Mix

Valid and extensive information on the environment and the current state of the organization is only one aspect of how information contributes to the design of competitive strategy. Information and information technology are also resources that can be deployed along with capital, labor, and other resources in the strategy design mix.

In spite of the millions of dollars and thousands of hours spent designing competitive strategies, most companies end up with strategies that sound remarkably alike. At the end of the day, everyone is interested in high-quality, low-cost products that meet or exceed customer requirements. And everyone recognizes the unattractiveness of competition based solely on price, so most companies strive to add value to justify higher prices and margins. The first page of virtually every strategic plan therefore contains something like the following:

XYZ, Inc. will be the world's foremost supplier of high-quality, low-cost gray gizmos, providing high value added for our customers, superior returns for our stockholders, and rewarding jobs for our employees.

Such a statement of "vision" is often developed following several senior management retreats, under the guidance of a consultant, with discussion and argument. And not surprisingly, it is ignored, considered irrelevant by most employees.

A good strategy design must get beyond such platitudes and satisfy at least these four criteria:

1. It must be distinctive, or at least it must show how the company will distinguish itself from its rivals. It is curious that few companies subject their strategy to a kind of "reverse engineering" to see how distinctive it really might be. One consulting firm, for example, built its strategy on three principles—superior people, strong client relationships, and breadth of practice—which suggests that the competition must have decided to hire stupid people with narrow specialities who go out of their way to irritate clients!

2. It must explicitly guide important tradeoffs (e.g., does the management of XYZ want lower cost or higher quality when push comes to shove?).

3. It must explicitly consider the competitive environment, including customers, suppliers, and competitors (e.g., does XYZ think gray gizmos are the only product it will ever make?).

4. It must explicitly consider all the resources that will be necessary to implement the strategy, including capital, human knowledge and capabilities, and **information**.

To some extent, the role of information in competitive strategy design is simply a matter of perspective. For example, a consumer finance company can think of itself as a financial intermediary, and its strategy would be concerned with issues of financing, lending practices, and so on. From this point of view, information is a by-product of the flow of capital from markets to borrowers. What the company doesn't have here is an explicit recognition of the information components of its business. On the other hand, if the company thinks of itself as an information company, then the focus shifts to concerns about information availability, the comparative advantage the company's information provides relative to the competition, and the human capabilities that will be necessary to take advantage of that information. In the latter perspective, the flow of capital is a by-product of the flow of information.

There is a duality about information that makes it difficult to generalize how it can be used strategically:

1. Information is both in surfeit and shortage at the same time. On the one hand, planners and strategists are bombarded with information from every quarter, and it has been said that the total knowledge in the world is now doubling every five years. On the other hand, there is clearly a shortage of the *right* information. For example, while many manufacturers recognize the need for clear information about customers' perceptions of their products and services (customer satisfaction measures), this information is only available in a few limited industries, most notably in the automobile industry, where the J. D. Powers' surveys are emerging as an authoritative source of customer satisfaction information. To obtain this information for other industries requires additional data gathering, which adds to information overload.

2. Information is difficult to create, yet easy to reproduce. On the one hand, *War and Peace* can be duplicated by a publisher millions of times without reducing its value. And in that sense, information is very highly leveragable. On the other hand, the work of creating *War and Peace* in the first place cannot be leveraged at all. One man had to sit and scratch out the ideas and concepts on his own with almost no leverage. Thus, it might be said that information creation is individual, while information dissemination can be leveraged.

3. Information only has real value when it is proprietary, for example, the copyright to *War and Peace*. Yet, information only has real economic value when it is shared. This seeming paradox must be resolved by finding a workable balance between maintaining proprietary rights and control over information, and sharing that information to gain the economic benefit of the information.

4. Information doesn't depreciate in the way that capital assets depreciate. In some circumstances, the value of information lasts forever: it's as valuable tomorrow as it is today. In other circumstances, the value of some kinds of information can drop to zero almost instantly when a certain event occurs. "As useless as yesterday's news," has real meaning in this context.

Many organizations still do not consider information at all during the strategy design process. A growing number consider information at the end of the design process as a sort of second-class resource that is relevant only in the execution of strategies. Leading organizations have elevated information to the same level as other critical resources, such as capital and labor. They pursue a strategy design process that considers information and information technology capabilities as a key design variable from the outset (Figure 1-3). In this alignment model, strategy alternatives inform and are informed by technology and information design alternatives.

Information and Strategy Execution

Implicit or explicit, carefully designed or ad hoc, competitive strategy is manifested in specific organizational processes that transform various inputs and resources (capital, technology,

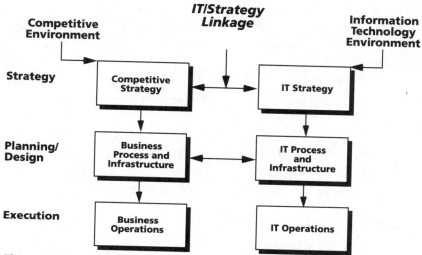

Figure 1.3   *Strategy Alignment Model*

labor, raw materials, etc.) into output products and services that provide value to customers. Porter's strategy model describes these processes as a *value chain* (Figure 1-4) connecting buyers and suppliers. But, organizations had been applying information technology to improve the efficiency and effectiveness of these processes long before strategists identified value chains.

Recently, organizations have begun to think about the opportunity inherent in explicitly designing the value-adding processes of the organization to take full advantage of the potentials of information technology. Prior to this explicit attention, however, a handful of organizations achieved competitive success from the application of information technology to their business processes. These applications established that information technology could play a significant role in creating significant competitive advantage.

When initially reported, these applications were taken as proof of the strategic potential of information technology. With distance and greater perspective, the role of information

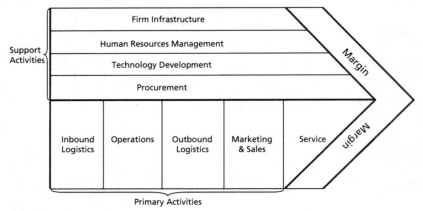

Figure 1.4   *The Value Chain*

technology in these applications is assuming a secondary role to that of information and process design.

A handful of companies have achieved near mythical status as exemplars of the use of information technology for competitive advantage. Four of these examples—American Airlines, Rosenbluth Travel, American Hospital Supply, and Frito-Lay—are worth revisiting in order to understand the lessons perspective provides to those organizations that would like comparable success.

American Airlines.   The heart of American Airlines' reputation in the information technology field lies in the story of the Sabre passenger reservation system. Originally developed for internal use and later offered to independent travel agencies, Sabre used emerging database and telecommunications technology to centralize information about passenger flight reservations and make this information accessible to operating staff throughout the organization (and subsequently to individuals outside the organization). American's explicit goal with the Sabre system was to improve operating efficiency by having more timely and more accurate information about seats booked for particular flights. Over time, Sabre was offered as a commercial service to travel agents, and information on the connecting flights of rival airlines was added to the system.

While most major airlines implemented on-line reservation systems, only American and United used them as part of their overall marketing strategies. Both American and United aggressively promoted the use of their systems by travel agents, and sought to obtain exclusive rights to the reservation business of given agents. Some competitors sued both American and United, charging them with bias in the way that their reservations systems displayed information about available flights. Competitors claimed that the reservation systems were designed to deliberately display all available information for American (or United) flights before displaying information for competitors' flights. Competitors argued that this "display bias" provided an advantage to the airline running the reservation system because travelers and travel agents tended to choose the first flight listed rather than review all possible flight options. As airline deregulation increased the role and importance of travel agents, American and United were perceived to have an "unfair" competitive advantage over other airlines in their control over access to travel agents. Competitors also complained about the costs and technical difficulties of providing flight information to these reservation systems.

Analyzed from the perspective of Porter's competitive strategy framework, American and United's reservation systems are examples of the use of information technology to create entrance barriers. As examples, they also demonstrate the importance of first mover advantages in deploying technology innovations. Less emphasized in early analyses was the careful integration of the use of information technology with larger marketing strategies, and the willingness of American and United to make sustained investments in developing and refining the technology of reservation systems.

American's experience with Sabre is also instructive in several other respects—some *information* rather than *information technology* oriented. American has continually sought to identify additional uses of the information captured by Sabre, and to find ways to exploit this information. For example, American was the first airline to introduce a frequent flier program, which became possible by reorganizing the information collected by Sabre in order to tally that information by person rather than flight. Later, American used the information collected in Sabre to drive statistical analyses of flight-load factors in order to support greater differentiation in pricing airline tickets. Recently, the same information base was used to support a marketing strategy for simplifying ticket pricing.

All of these examples suggest that American Airlines has understood the relative importance of information and technology, emphasizing the exploitation of information. American has also successfully created a management environment that recognizes the importance of continuing to combine innovation and information.

Rosenbluth Travel.   Rosenbluth Travel provides an interesting illustration of a competitor whose information-enabled strategies do not operate in a vacuum anymore than any other dimension of strategy. While American Airlines was using its investments in reservation systems to improve its strategic positioning, Rosenbluth was investing in information-enabled strategies to counter those moves and advance its own strategic agenda.

Rather than accept a reservation system from a single carrier, Rosenbluth opted to develop its own system for direct customer interaction. Rosenbluth took data feeds from multiple carriers into a back office system, which then supported a custom-developed front office system. While other travel agents were at the mercy of American or United for presenting flight information in whatever format or sequence made most sense for the airline, Rosenbluth, on the other hand, used its own systems to present the combined carrier information. It used its back office computer systems to search through all available flight information, and identify and guarantee the lowest available fare to its customers. For the businesses Rosenbluth's marketing strategy targeted, this service was highly valued.

This strategy did not require inordinate investments in information technology. It did require Rosenbluth to negotiate different arrangements with the airlines about providing data feeds on fares and flight information. It also required Rosenbluth to invest more heavily in training its reservation agents to use its systems. However, this training investment was also part of broader efforts by Rosenbluth to maintain high levels of service quality.

As with American Airlines, Rosenbluth's initial commitments to an information-enabled strategy have also led to a continuing need to seek out and invest in new uses of the information that it maintained. For example, Rosenbluth uses its automated systems to check whether its quality standards are being met. Systems cross-check passenger reservation records against passenger profiles to see whether a particular reservation meets special requests (e.g., seating preferences or special meals), recorded in the profile.

American Hospital Supply. It is not clear whether American Hospital Supply or American Airlines has become the most overworked example of information technology and strategy. Both continue to offer important lessons, however, particularly as greater knowledge about these stories gains value with time and perspective.

Beginning in the early 1970s, American Hospital (since acquired by Baxter) created an information system that allowed purchasing managers in hospitals to directly enter orders into American Hospital's computer systems. In this system, American Hospital supplied its customers with computer terminals (later with personal computers) that were directly connected to American Hospital's central computers. Instead of calling a sales representative, customers would take direct responsibility for entering their orders. As with the airline reservation systems, the initial strategic analysis was that American Hospital had managed to lock in customers and create entrance barriers to potential competitors. Customers would be unwilling to switch to another supplier because of the time and effort already invested in learning how to use the system.

The full story, of course, is richer. American Hospital was only one of many hospital suppliers who provided terminals for their order entry systems. But American Hospital offered the broadest line of items, making it the most attractive supplier with whom to place orders. Also, American Hospital did not use its system to eliminate sales representatives. Instead, its sales representatives worked with hospital purchasing managers to increase their ability to manage inventories and costs at a time of rising attention to cost management in the health care industry.

Also, over time, American Hospital has made continuing investments and improvements in its order entry systems. What began as an effort to create an information system to support the company's broad-line distribution strategy has evolved into an electronic marketplace to link hospital purchasing managers with many supplies' manufacturers. More importantly, from the earliest implementations of American Hospital's order entry system, there has been conscious attention paid to jointly developing business processes that integrate the company's order processing with the order management processing of its customers. These kinds of mutually beneficial activities are becoming increasingly common, and can be termed "electronic commerce," which is discussed at greater length in Chapter 3.

Frito-Lay. Frito-Lay offers an example of efforts to increase efficiencies and control in core sales and distribution processes, which bring initial benefits as well as gradual changes in broader marketing and management processes. Frito-Lay's long-term distribution strategy has been direct store delivery of its products. In the mid-1980s Frito equipped its truck drivers with handheld computing technology that recorded sales and inventory information for every customer account on a given route. The handheld computers replaced a paper intensive process that was prone to errors and abuse. The paper accounting process also diverted drivers' time from selling tasks to internal paperwork.

Frito offers an example of a well-managed effort to change day-to-day operating processes by introducing new technology capabilities. It also offers an example of the clear-cut economic benefits of being open to opportunities presented by continuing improvements in underlying information technologies.

Frito-Lay also offers some important lessons about strategic benefits that flow from improving the quality of information created while executing core business processes. The Frito-Lay system captures data about fundamental business events such as, how many bags of potato chips were sold to a particular A&P store. Further, this data is captured immediately in machine-readable form. While there are immediate benefits from the efficiency of this use of technology, there are equal or greater benefits from the availability of this data for interpretation and analysis. With raw event data captured consistently and accurately, Frito's sales and marketing managers are now able to discuss and debate marketing strategy alternatives from a base of common facts that all managers share and agree on. With a single source of data, marketing review meetings can focus on substantive debates on strategy instead of arguments over the "facts."

Information-Enabled Competitive Strategies

Each of these examples offers lessons on the importance of information—frequently enabled by advancing technology—for the ability of organizations to execute their business strategies in the processes that create and deliver products and services. From this point of view, competitive strategy is an information map that answers questions about how the company will operate in an information intensive world. What information *must* an organization have, and capitalize on better than anyone else, regarding customers, competitors, and competitive environment? What information *must* organizations provide to customers or suppliers, and how will they use it (and combine it with their own information) to provide superior inputs to the organization? How can organizations embed information into existing products and services, and how might these be developed into information products? These are the questions that a competitive information strategy must address.

Resources and Capabilities— Core Competences

Although Porter's strategy frameworks provide powerful tools for strategy design, they do not translate directly into guidance for strategy execution. The notion of "core competence," introduced by Hamel and Prahalad,[2] provides this link. Core competences place knowledge and information at the heart of the linkage between strategy and execution. Core competences are not things that an organization must own, but things that an organization must know. From a strategy design perspective, McDonald's would be described as a company with good store locations, reliable suppliers, innovative products, and so on. But McDonald's core competencies could be described as the ability to *find* good locations, *control* the reliability of suppliers, and *understand* customers' changing tastes for new products. Focusing core competencies explicitly on the information necessary to execute design extends the notion in a useful way. While the difference may seem subtle, the focus on information and knowledge moves away from a static description of the company today, toward a dynamic process of innovation and improvement.

Information and Integration

Information affects strategy design both as a central input to the design process and as a key design variable. Information and information technology have been used to significant competitive advantage in the execution of core business processes. The third role for information is as the link between design and execution. This linkage serves two purposes. First, the link serves as a feedback loop to ensure that execution is being carried out in alignment with the strategy design. Second, the link provides the source of information through which an organization can learn and adapt its strategies to the competitive environment.

As Figure 1-5 suggests, a strategy must simultaneously consider a vision of the company's **position** relative to the competitive environment, the **resources and capabilities** that will

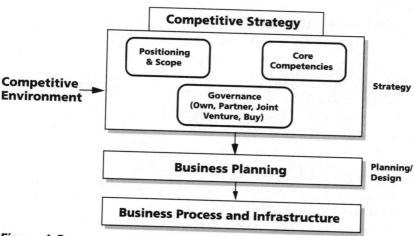

Figure 1.5   *Key Dimensions of Competitive Strategy*

be necessary to develop and sustain that position, and the way the organization will be **structured and governed** to achieve that position.

Where the previous section discussed the *business process dimension* of strategy execution, "structure and governance" reflect the *management process dimension* of strategy. In the classic, *Organization and Environment*, Paul Lawrence and Jay Lorsch argue that organizations respond to environmental complexity by differentiating into specialized units that must then be held together, or integrated, toward a common set of objectives. Hierarchical structure is the most common mechanism for integration, by providing a tool for transmitting information throughout the organization. Information functions as the "glue" that holds the organization together. In fact, in most large organizations, an essential function of "middle management" has been to enable this information transmission.

Middle managers, however, are the *transmitters* of the information "glue"; they are not the glue itself. Thus, as organizations have begun to look for productivity advances, they have turned toward this middle layer of management. If one explicitly recognizes the informational role these layers of management play, it often becomes possible to remove the layers by transmitting required information directly from provider to user. If this direct transmission does not happen, however, removal of the intermediate layers will create an information gap between senior management and lower-level employees that might be termed, "delamination."

The performance measurement, or feedback, dimension of information and strategy operates in two directions. Moving forward from design to execution, organizations must more effectively communicate the relevant aspects of strategy design to the appropriate stakeholders and resource providers to the organization. A strategy whose design depends on improving the quality of purchased parts for manufacturing purposes has to communicate that goal both to suppliers and purchasing agents in the organization. Core competences help to identify specific behaviors in the organization that are appropriate to the strategy design.

Performance measurement systems must establish the processes, measurement infrastructure, and performance reporting systems that will inform both senior executives and managers throughout the organization that the execution activities called for in the strategy design are, in fact, occurring. For instance, are purchasing agents being measured, promoted, and rewarded based on cost savings, while the strategy calls for quality?

All organizations have multiple performance measurement and reporting systems. Some, such as financial accounting systems, are mandated by external regulatory authorities. Others are created to meet special needs, such as project reporting and budgeting systems. Despite the proliferation of measurement efforts within organizations, few have designed systems whose explicit goal is to create the bridge between strategy design and execution.

In a static or slow-changing competitive environment, once design, execution and integration have been put in place, the job is done. In the dynamic environment most organizations face today, however, an appropriate fit for today will not be appropriate for tomorrow. Learning is the organizational process that manages the continual adaptation of the organization to its environment. In a highly dynamic environment, learning processes must be consciously and explicitly managed to reduce the risk of potentially fatal gaps between the environment and the organization.

Notes

1. Prahalad, C.K. and G. Hamel (1990), "The Core Competence of the Organization," *Harvard Business Review*. 68(3):118–125.

2. Hamel G. and C.K. Prahalad (1989), "Strategic Intent," *Harvard Business Review*. 67(3):63–76.

PART II

Information
and
Strategy
Design

The first part of competitive strategy is the design problem of articulating a combination of resources and activities that will position the organization's products and services to stand out in the competitive environment. The problems of designing and crafting effective strategy have received a great deal of attention over the past twenty years. There is widespread agreement on the essential elements of strategy design. How and where should information fit into this process?

First, the strategy design process is an information intensive process in its own right. Effective design requires accurate and timely information in large volumes and variety. Although providing volumes of data to strategy design is already the norm, it is not clear whether these provisions possess the requisite variety and diversity for success in today's economic environment. Presently there are more ways to compete, more threats, and more opportunities in the external environment than ever. At the same time, strategy designers need a better grasp on internal strengths and weaknesses to match against such threats and opportunities. All of this demands information. As a critical organizational process, strategy design can benefit more than most organizational processes from the information management practices described in Part II.

Information also needs to be treated with the same seriousness as any other strategic resource. Chapter 2 works through the implications of using information as a strategic resource. Information provides a double opportunity by offering new strategy design choices of its own, and by creating ways to leverage conventional strategy design choices in new and unexpected ways.

Although there are many information and information technology trends that have implications for strategy design, most fall into the category of understanding the implications of "better, faster, and cheaper." One especially important trend, however, is the gradual and largely quiet trend toward a world of "electronic commerce." More and more of the routine, day-to-day, interaction between organizations is occurring electronically. Chapter 3 explores the gradual emergence of electronic commerce and its implications for strategy design and execution. It focuses in particular on how a pervasively interconnected business environment will require organizations to seek a new balance between the pursuit of competitive advantage and the pursuit of "cooperative advantage."

2

The Role of
Information in
Strategy Design

The strategy alignment model introduced in the previous chapter elevates information as a resource to be considered during the strategy design process to a level that is equivalent to traditional strategy design choices such as product/service positioning, manufacturing strategy, channel strategy, and financing strategy. What does it mean to include information and information technology as variables in the strategy design process?

Elements of Strategy Design

As Figure 2-1 indicates, there are three elements in the strategy design process of creating a viable organization in the competitive environment, and each focuses on a different critical issue; positioning and scope, core competences, and governance. Each design element is supported both by an evolving base of research and practical experience. Each has an evolving set of design principles and heuristics, which guide the articulation of strategy. For each, the contribution and impact of information and information technology must be addressed.

There is one important difference about information compared to other strategy design variables: information can operate as a design variable in two distinct ways. First, information and information technology can be used to *leverage* more conventional design variables such as product differentiation. Second, information and information technology can be used directly to *invent* new strategy choices.

Positioning and Scope

Positioning and scope is concerned with articulating products and services that can be distinguished in the marketplace either through unique characteristics or compelling economies of scale or scope. Porter's work offers two models that have

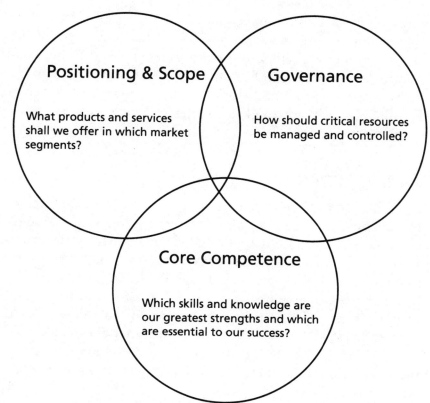

Figure 2.1 *Elements of Strategy Design*

been widely adopted for evaluating design choices of positioning and scope. The industry analysis framework in Chapter 1 (Figure 1-1) provides an analytic framework for evaluating the company in the context of its environment. Strategy design choices can be considered in terms of their ability to alter the balance of power between suppliers and customers, and their ability to alter entrance barriers among industries. The value chain (Figure 1-4) provides a framework for evaluating design choices in terms of how resources are configured into processes for actually creating a company's products and services.

If information is a strategic resource equal to labor, capital, or technology, these models will apply. Information and information technology can be analyzed in terms of their ability to contribute to changes in the relative bargaining power of customers and suppliers; to create, remove, or sidestep barriers to entry; and to differentiate companies from their industry rivals. Information also offers new alternatives for configuring value chains and achieving differing economies of scale and scope.

Governance

Governance is a term that is gaining favor in research circles. It encompasses a number of critical issues in strategy design about how organizations are designed and controlled to ensure the execution of strategy. Governance is concerned with a simple question—Who's in charge here? Traditionally, goverance has addressed questions of vertical integration and joint ventures. Which skills or resources are important enough to a company's strategy that they must be under the company's direct control? Figure 2-2 summarizes the essential questions that need to be addressed in designing appropriate governance structures.

Information and information technology are becoming particularly important in the potential strategic contributions of governance choices. New capabilities for exchanging and communicating information have added degrees of freedom in choices about the structure and form of organizations. These new freedoms imply that governance choices must be explicitly considered and evaluated during the strategy design process.

Core Competences

Core competence explicitly considers the knowledge and skills possessed by companies as an element of their strategy design alternatives. The concept has grown from research on how companies implement their other strategy design choices—po-

Source: John C. Henderson

Figure 2.2   *Elements of Governance Design*

sitioning and scope, and governance. Whereas choices of positioning and scope focus on how a company is perceived by its customers, core competence frames design choices in terms of the strengths a company must possess in order to deliver those choices of positioning and scope. Figure 2-3 illustrates how core competence relates to other perspectives on strategy design.

At some level, core competence and information are synonymous. Both are about the skills and knowledge held by the members of the organization, and the ability of the organization to tap this knowledge to create value. Issues of positioning and scope, as well as issues of governance, are discussed in detail in this chapter. Core competence issues are implied

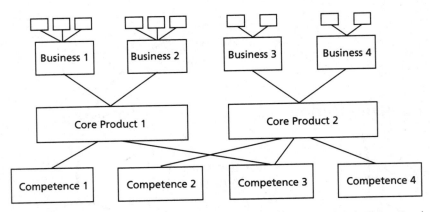

Figure 2.3   *Core Competence Perspective*

in the sections that discuss strategy execution and the linkage between design and execution. In some ways, this book extends the definition of core competence, and gives it preeminence in terms of particular design issues.

New Positioning and Scope Alternatives Made Available by Information

Information-Leveraged Differentiation

Differentiation had been a fundamental goal of strategy design long before Porter elevated it to the status of a basic, generic strategy. Creating products and services that customers deem unique is becoming increasingly important in today's business climate, which has been reemphasizing quality. Information plays an especially important role in leveraging efforts to create and sustain differentiation. At the point of interaction between the company and a customer, information is a central tool for individualizing customer service in an anonymous world. Pushed further, this tailoring of customer service evolves into a market pluralism of information-leveraged and -enabled niche markets in which niches have the potential of having only a single occupant.

Individuated Customer Service—
19th-Century Service
in the 21st Century

Individuated customer service is built on the notion that consumers are increasingly demanding to be treated as individuals, not just members of a large group. High quality service, more and more, is coming to mean that the service provider and the customer interact on the basis of (apparently) personal knowledge of each other's background, experience, and needs. In essence, we are seeking the 19th-century experience of the shopkeeper who knew each customer personally—but on the global scale of the 21st century.

It is all very interesting that Nordstrom's hires and rewards sales people who politely and efficiently serve their customers who trade in the local store. Much more important to Nordstrom's long term success, however, is the ability to provide this same kind of service to customers who normally shop at the Nordstrom's in Seattle, but who are visiting San Francisco—to know that the tie you buy to match your suit will match three other suits in your wardrobe.

Currently this information about individual customer preferences is resident only in the memory of each sales associate. What is needed is for this information to be converted from personal memory to corporate memory.

Face-to-face customer service can be enhanced through more attention to the individual characteristics of the customer on the other side of the counter. Hertz's Gold Club demonstrates that customers want this personal attention (we know exactly what you want, so just take the car and be off), so much so that customers are willing to pay an extra $50 for the privilege.

The mass markets of the industrial economy depended on the standardization of products, "one size fits all." We gave up the individuated information of the local shopkeeper for the group information of mass merchants. In a capital-based economy, the loss of information was not a problem given the increase in efficient use of the capital. Mass production economies made products available to a market that could not even contemplate the cost of custom-manufactured products. There was no incentive to understand the unique requirements of individual customers, even if there had been a possibility of offering a customized product. Today, the situation has reversed. The availability of mass-produced products is taken for granted. Now, the unique characteristics of products and services become paramount and information must be considered the central resource.

It is very difficult for a large department store to provide individuated service when the sales assistant and the customer have never met before, will not likely meet again, and have no common knowledge about the customer's requirements, prior purchases, likes, dislikes, and so on. Yet, demographic trends suggest that there will be fewer and fewer people to provide face-to-face customer service, despite the fact that consumers are demanding more personalized interaction. Differentiation will increasingly depend on the quality of this interaction, and the quality of interaction will be enhanced by efficient capture, storage, and sharing of customer information.

Consider how many executives enjoy being recognized by name at the local restaurant, country club, or a well-known hotel. To some extent, it is a mark of having arrived. And yet, companies don't take that prescription to work when thinking about how customer service might be improved.

Improving the quality of face-to-face interaction comes from two sources:

1. Acquiring and delivering information at the "point of" interaction. While it may be true that Hertz recorded all of your auto rental habits over many years, this information is of marginal value to the provision of individuated services if it is not delivered at the counter where you rent the car. With this information, the service provider can know about the customer at the time of interaction.

   American Airlines has information about your flights.[1] By providing that information to the gate agent, they can greet you individually, ask about recent flights, and, recognizing the importance of having repeat business travelers, they can provide special treatment for good customers, and generally treat each of their passengers as a separate bundle of "needs and desires."

2. Creating and maintaining a "corporate memory" to replace the individual memories that were lost in the mass market. The 19th-century shopkeeper had a personal memory. He knew you and your family, and you shared a common heritage and history. But, of course, he could only maintain this information for a limited number of customers. As his business grew, his ability to keep track of this information for all customers diminished. With hundreds of thousands of customers spread out on a world-wide scale, the only way to provide that same kind of service is to have the same information for those customers as well. The questions an executive must answer are:

   What information do we want to gather and maintain about our customers, and how will that information be delivered and used by the service provider?

In other words, what kind of "corporate memory" do we want to develop?

Market Pluralism—From Mass Market to Information Niche

Over the last couple of decades we have seen the death of mass markets for standardized goods, at least in the industrial world. There is an interesting problem here, because customers essentially want customized goods and services at mass-produced prices. The notion of mass-produced essentially means that one makes the same product for large numbers of consumers, while custom-produced products provide peculiar bundles of benefits that satisfy particular customer's needs. Again, it is important to note that mass production is characteristic of a situation where large capital investments are leveraged through scale economies to achieve low unit costs. All else equal, to use an economist's favorite simplifying assumption, a product tailored to your individual needs is preferable. Scale economies drive the costs of standard products so low that most customers are willing to accept, however grudgingly, these standard products.

The conundrum, of course, is that customization reduces the efficiency of production, and increases costs. You can either have a car made to unique specifications at a very high cost, or you can buy a Ford Taurus that has a limited set of options (and, based on the number of them on the highway, one that is probably blue). Historically, the distinction has been between very expensive, "bespoke" products and much lower cost, "off the rack" products. It will become increasingly necessary to produce highly customized products without foregoing the cost benefits of mass production techniques. Essentially, business is getting to the point where every customer is a niche.

Information is at the heart of these attempts to achieve

market pluralism. For example, efforts to achieve mass customization in manufacturing by implementing flexible manufacturing strategies are all enabled by information-intensive technologies. Information and knowledge embedded in computer-aided manufacturing technologies achieve economies comparable to the scale economies that drove mass production strategies during the industrial revolution. Conventional manufacturing technologies achieve scale economies by maximizing production time and minimizing setup and changeover time. Setup and changeover time is where the information and knowledge of production workers is "programmed" into the tooling of the manufacturing technology. Flexible manufacturing technologies use information technology to embed this same information and knowledge into the machines themselves, reducing the importance of scale economies.

Hand-crafted and customized products are valued because of the knowledge embedded in them. This knowledge is of two types. First, there is the knowledge and expertise of the craftsperson, embodied in the quality of the product. German engineering is the archetypal form of this product quality. Years of practical experience and expertise—information—are embedded in the final product's fit and finish. This information is acquired by and resides in the heads of individual craftspeople and engineers.

The Japanese have adopted an alternative strategy of embedding similar levels of information in their quality products. Rather than rely on the skills and knowledge of individuals, the Japanese built the same knowledge and information into the production system. Individuals still create the knowledge and expertise out of their experience, but it is shared with the organizational system.

The second way that knowledge is embedded in customized products is through the knowledge of individual customers and their needs and desires. More malleable than plastic and steel, information content can be used to create the customized characteristics of a product.

Increasingly, information-as-product is emerging as the ultimate expression of market pluralism. Separating out the information components from the other constituents of a product or service allows organizations to create new combinations of information and, hence, new products. J. D. Powers, for example, has built a business on collecting and selling information about customer preferences. Companies spend hundreds of millions of dollars purchasing data from other companies; data on customer purchases, demographic and census data, and data on market share, to name a handful of examples. In the financial services industries, the entire product development process has become one of identifying and packaging information to sell.

Information and Scale and Scope Economies

If you can't make a product that is unique, the alternative is to make it for less. Economies of *scale and scope* can be as important to strategic success as differentiation. Porter identifies low cost as a generic strategy equal in importance to differentiation. Although Porter argues that cost and differentiation are competing and contradictory strategy design choices, few companies have paid much heed. Whether theoretically questionable or not, most companies seek to strike a balance between differentiation and economies. Information is changing this balance in important and unexpected ways.

Scale advantages exist when large fixed costs for plant, marketing, and the like are spread over a large number of units. In the case of scale economy, the fixed costs are spread over the number of units produced, while in the case of scope economy, costs are spread over the number of different products. In either case, large capital investments in plant, equipment, distribution channel, and so on were made to produce large numbers of units very efficiently. The only way to compete was to make the requisite investment. Success went to the company that could make the largest capital investments and, therefore, achieve the lowest costs per unit.

Eliminating Barriers to Entry with Information

If the industrial revolution was driven by the substitution of capital for labor, the information revolution substitutes information for capital. Operating on different assumptions, it sidesteps advantages built on conventional economic assumptions.

Take the business of consumer automobile lending. Traditionally, these loans were sold through local branches of commercial banks. Like most retailers, the banks did not often go to the customer, they waited for the customer to come to them. Therefore, from a strategy design point of view, a critical variable in the auto lending business was the number and location of branches—if you were close to the customer, you would get your share of the auto lending business (assuming comparable capital costs). How could anyone compete with Bank of America in California, for example, with its thousands of branches and millions of customers?

The answer was to recast the problem in information terms. A lending transaction still has scale economies in terms of the ability to obtain funds to lend at favorable rates. But the information problem is twofold: first, to obtain data about prospective borrowers to evaluate their ability to repay the loan; second, to gain access to prospective borrowers. The availability of information about borrowers has increased steadily with the growth of credit reporting services such as TRW and Equifax. This offsets any information a bank may have had from possessing knowledge about its customers financial history.

With the critical information ingredient to effectively evaluate prospective borrowers, the scale barrier of a branch network can be offset by bringing the transaction to the customer.

Any company with information about consumer credit and low-cost capital could simply hire (on commission) a salesperson at the dealership to peddle auto loans. Without the brick and mortar capital costs of a large branch network, the loans could be made more cheaply and more profitably. In effect, the large consumer automobile lenders (GMAC, GE Credit, etc.) used information to overcome a traditional entrance barrier—the cost of a branch network.

Reebok offers another example of using information to avoid large capital investments, and exercise control over productive resources without ownership. Reebok uses superior information about consumer shoe requirements and product design to meet those needs, to compete in the athletic footwear business without actually manufacturing shoes. In many ways, Reebok is a pure information company, differentiating on the basis of what it knows rather than its investment in capital intensive facilities and equipment.

Creating Barriers to Entry with Information

Information and information technology can also be used to create barriers to entry. As much as one-third of current U.S. capital investment is in the form of new information technology.[2] With the price tag of complex information systems reaching into the tens of millions of dollars, the size of information technology investments can become a potential barrier to entry.

Merrill Lynch's invention of the cash management account is sometimes cited as an example of a strategic information system. This innovation represented a significant capital investment on Merrill Lynch's part; an investment that few organizations are capable of making. While the sheer size of the investment operates as a barrier to entry, Merrill Lynch achieved further barrier-oriented benefits after the system was operational.

Once the initial cash management account was announced by Merrill Lynch, they gained market share at the expense of their competitors as customers shifted accounts to them to take advantage of the CMA account. This forced competitors to implement and offer comparable accounts to the market. Although competitors had the advantage of duplicating Merrill Lynch's cash management account, they were forced to do so on a crash implementation basis, incurring incremental costs. Thus, information technology investments can be used as one element of a strategy to force competitors to respond to innovations with duplicate systems. While this may raise overall costs and reduce profitability within an industry, another possibility for competitors with significant investment resources may be to drive some competitors from the field.

Redesigning Value Chains

Information changes scale and scope economies by making new choices possible in the design of value chains. The value chain (Figure 1-4) is an analytic tool with which to organize the design of the value-adding activities within an organization in order to transform inputs into products and services. Scale and scope economies are created in the way the organizations designed their value chains and chose which activities to organize and control internally.

Information allows competitors to break down the value chain, and rebuild it in new and different ways using information linkages. Reebok is also an instructive example of a company that used its information-based expertise to achieve levels of efficiency similar to those of fully integrated rivals without significantly investing, like the rivals. It is not necessary to have enormous manufacturing facilities to be in the shoe business. It is only necessary to have proprietary information about manufacturer and customer demand, and to match buyers and sellers. In fact, large manufacturing facilities may become a strategic hindrance in situations in which flexibility begins to dominate low cost.

In the configuration of a value chain, design choices organize resources subject to constraints of time and space. Information can alter and eliminate these limits. It is no longer necessary to be physically contiguous with customers in order to assess their needs, or to deliver products to them. GE Credit Corporation, for example, makes auto loans without ever seeing their customers.

Several publishers now offer services to college professors that allow them to custom-publish textbooks for their classes. These systems exploit information and information technology in two ways. First, the publishers use information to assemble and access necessary copyrights and permissions. Second, publishers use information technology to store the text material in machine-readable form. The actual printing is left to local printers who can deliver the actual material to students at relatively low cost. By extension, this specialized form of textbook publishing could be offered by any company who has the information expertise to keep track of availability, copyrights, and the like on a global scale, without regard to physical location of the business. Thus, in the year 2000, textbook publishing (if textbooks of any kind still exist) could easily be dominated by a company in Singapore, Ireland, or anywhere else that information expertise exists.

Information and Governance Alternatives

Questions of governance and competitive strategy have principally interested academic researchers until recently. But improvements in information and communication technologies have led to a more practical role for governance in strategy design.

Value chain design decomposes the organization into discrete skills, processes, and functions needed to create its products and services. It is driven by the capacity limits of individuals and small groups to develop and maintain specific skills and knowledge. Governance concerns itself with how to assemble and control the discrete configurations of knowledge and skill to make up the complete value chain. It is intimately tied with broader issues of authority and control within organizations. From an information perspective, governance alternatives are driven by changing constraints in the ability to communicate across time and distance.

Traditionally, governance choices were limited to the use of hierarchical reporting and authority structures and to limited uses of alliances and joint ventures when particular strategies exceeded the productive capacities of a single organization. Information and information technologies have made alternatives to hierarchical reporting and authority feasible. Further, organizations are choosing to design strategies that exceed the capacities and competences of a single organization. Information-enabled changes in internal organization are discussed in the next section. The impact of information and information technology on relationships across organizations is discussed in the next chapter.

Alternatives to Hierarchical Command and Control

The hierarchical chain of command has been the quintessential organizational tool since the 19th century. Adopted from the military, it is an information processing tool designed to mesh the needs for control of senior executives with the limited information processing capacity of individual managers. From the top down, hierarchy filters, summarizes, and reduces masses of detailed data into an integrated picture that senior managers can use to make strategy and set policy. From the bottom up, hierarchy circumscribes and limits the information processing responsibilities of each member in the chain of command. As an information processing technology, hierarchy remains a remarkably effective tool for managing complexity. It has weaknesses, however. Too often, it reinforces an implicit assumption that information and intelligence is located only at the top of the pyramid.

The Cold War produced a curious example of this problem of hierarchy. The chain of command is particularly important in the military, and the communication systems of U.S. military services reflect this hierarchy. The telephone and teletype systems of the military were designed for generals to talk quickly to other generals and colonels. Messages from the lower ranks had to filter their way up the chain of command. The imminent threat of nuclear war, however, created unique problems for communications systems. Generals (and many others) wanted to know as quickly as possible whether a nuclear attack was taking place. What if a private was the first to see the mushroom cloud? The solution was to create a "flash" override. Anyone could send a message straight to the top by invoking a "flash override." Of course, the sanctions for unauthorized use were severe.

On a more prosaic level, software development companies such as Borland and Microsoft depend critically on the free flow of information. Both rely heavily on electronic mail systems, and their CEOs send and receive messages from any level in their organizations.

Generic Information Strategies

Just as there are generic approaches to strategy in the broad area of competitive strategy, there are generalizable approaches to the use of information and information technology as strategic resources. We've been discussing the use of information in the context of generic competitive strategies. What generic information strategies are emerging?

We see the emergence of three generic information strategies: the **information-leverage** strategy, the **information-product** strategy, and the **information-business** strategy (Figure 2-4). With the information-leverage strategy, the focus is on the development of proprietary information capabilities for internal use. This is a strategy that can and should be pursued

Generic Strategy	Distinguishing Features
Information-Leverage	Fundamental strategy built on traditional basis (e.g., economies of scale, product differentiation, etc.)
	Information technology permits significant process innovation or redesign
	Information technology amplifies competitive dimensions of underlying base strategy
Information-Product	Existing processes generate or capture significant volumes of data as a by-product of transaction processing
	Market for the by-product information is identified or created
	Product/service opportunities generated out of summarizing or massaging transaction processing information by-products
Information-Business	Excess capacity in internal information systems can be sold to other industry participants
	Clear market demand exists for specific information product or service (e.g., abstracting services or information brokers)

Figure 2.4 *Generic Information Strategies*

by any organization. The next two strategies, while important, only apply in more specialized circumstances, and may not be appropriate for all organizations.

Information Leverage Strategies

Leverage is the fundamental concept to the strategic use of information. Leverage can be gained at many levels—from the individual to cross-organizational. Value comes from explicitly considering how to increase performance at every level by leveraging the use of information—enabled with technology, as appropriate. In one industry after another, a company will take the lead in using information as a competitive weapon, and in the process, change the rules of competition for every-one. We call these dramatic changes "10X Improvements," because they often represent tenfold improvements for the innovator (often while rivals are satisfied with 10% annual gains).

American Airlines demonstrates a particularly important aspect of information-leverage strategies. American has used information to differentiate its services in many ways—making its reservation system available to travel agents, offering fre-quent flier programs and special ticket pricing, and most re-cently, attempting to simplify its fare structures.

There are two ways that American leverages these strat-egies through information. First, American is able to formulate and execute these strategies because of its investments in in-formation and the supporting information technology. A fre-quent flier program isn't possible until you've begun to collect and save information about flying habits. The speed and ca-pacity of information technology is necessary to make the pro-gram technically feasible. American has used its prior successes in information and information technology investments to cre-ate a positive feedback loop. American's skill at exploiting in-formation and technology begets more skill.

The second, more impressive aspect of American's use of

information is that it has used its ability to differentiate to create an entrance barrier for other competitors. As American accumulates greater information, and learns more about how to make use of this information, it becomes increasingly difficult for competitors to keep up. Although any individual technology investment might be copiable, the pattern of investments over time and American's organizational learning about how to leverage the information becomes increasingly difficult to emulate.

Information-Product Strategies

The information-product strategy builds upon the proprietary capability that is developed from leveraging information by seeking ways to embed information into existing products and services. With the information-product strategy, information is explicitly recognized as a critical part of the "product package" sold to customers. Traditionally, information, if it was considered at all, was seen as a by-product of a company's operation. It was not something that had value in its own right. It is increasingly clear, however, that future successful organizations will develop information enhancements to their products and services, and they will identify ways to satisfy customer needs by bundling, unbundling, and repackaging information with the products they sell.

American Express's Travel Related Services group offers one example of an information-product strategy. American Express collects and maintains immense amounts of data as a by-product of its credit card processing operations. Once the data has been collected, it can be repackaged and resold as other forms of information products. For corporate accounts, for example, charges can be summarized and reported by geography or type of expense. These represent additional opportunities by which to extract value from the information that has been collected as a part of the routine transaction processing activities of the organization.

Information-Business Strategies

Finally, the information-business strategy goes one step further by recognizing the value of the information in its own right, and develops a full-fledged business around the company's information capability. This, for example, is the logic behind American Airlines' creation of a separate subsidiary to manage its Sabre system and make the system available to other airlines. Other examples of new businesses built around the collection and sale of information multiply daily. The OAG, for example, which publishes information on airline schedules, has a higher market value than many of the airlines whose schedules it reports.

With the information-business strategy, companies can extend the notion of information value beyond their own boundaries. We believe the 1990s will see an explosion of information companies whose primary product is the acquisition, manipulation, or dissemination of proprietary information. Some of these firms, such as Dun & Bradstreet, Dow-Jones, and J. D. Powers, exist today and numerous others (probably highly specialized) will emerge over the next few years. Many, however, will grow out of existing companies that recognize the value of information they currently maintain and control for internal purposes.

Relationships Among Information Strategies

While there is certainly no "natural evolution" of these strategies from internal focus to external focus, there is some evidence that companies with an information-business strategy often begin with a more modest objective. A fast-food chain competing on the basis of superior site selection, for example, would probably initially focus on the architecture, design, and implementation of a world class "siting information capability," which would include identifying information sources, computerized and non-computerized storage and manipulation capabilities, sophisticated geographical analysis, and so on. As this capability develops, however, the company will almost certainly see ways to embed its proprietary information into the products and services it delivers (e.g., added information for franchisees, joint ventures to offer multiple products at the same desirable site, etc.). Ultimately, if the company is truly successful in creating a world-class repository of siting information, then it might begin to sell that information to other companies, probably at higher profit margins than the fast-food business that incited the development of the information capability in the first place.

Information-Enabled Competition

Information-enabled strategies present the greatest single opportunity, or threat, depending on your perspective, for companies to radically alter the basics of competitive balance. Specific advances in technology are far less important in this equation than developing a clear understanding of the design dimensions of an organization's strategy, and ways that technology can affect each design dimension.

Strategy design focuses on developing an artful match between an organization's core competences and its environment. A central element in this matching is detecting pertinent patterns or changes in the environment that can be exploited. One change of particular relevance to strategy design is the emergence of electronic commerce. As more and more organizations put information and information technology to use to implement strategies and support critical business processes, more and more economic activity between organizations is taking place electronically. The strategy design implications of this trend are considered in the next chapter.

Notes

1. Consultants write about airlines and rental car companies becaue they comprise a large portion of a consultant's working life.

2. Roach, Steven S. (1987). "America's Technology Dilemma: A Profile of the Information Economy." Morgan Stanley Special Economic Study, April 22, 1987.

3

Pursuing Cooperative Advantage in a World of Electronic Commerce

Today you can walk up to an automated teller machine in Heathrow airport and a few moments later walk away with cash drawn from your bank account in San Francisco. A merchant in Sydney, Australia can take your credit card, pass it through a reader attached to the cash register, and receive authorization from your bank in Massachusetts forty seconds later for the mask and snorkel you've just purchased. These events are already so commonplace that they elicit no reaction from the average consumer.

Behind the scenes, however, is a complex web of technology that moves the information from computer to computer—from merchant to bank to credit card company to bank, and back again—to complete one simple transaction. Alongside this technology web is a web of agreements and contracts integrating the organizations in their collective efforts to complete your single transaction. Well-advanced in the banking and financial services industries, this "electronic commerce" is reshaping the way organizations conduct their business with other organizations.

Introducing information technology into the routine activities that link one organization with another—creating interorganizational systems—is significantly more challenging than implementing information systems within the confines of the organization. In some situations, interorganizational systems have contributed to changes in competitive position. The strategic successes of American Airlines' Sabre system and American Hospital Supply's ASAP order-entry system are examples of the competitive advantage potential of interorganizational systems.

Discussions of such systems have focused on using information technology to create barriers to entry or to lock in customers by making it too difficult or undesirable to switch from one technologically supported business process to that of a competitor. The competitive logic, from the owner's point of view, is that the strategic advantage of these systems is derived from the investments that customers make to tailor their business processes in conformity with the system's embedded technology. Customers become locked in because it is too painful for them to contemplate the switching costs of abandoning one system for another vendor's equally unique system.

In other industries, most notably, grocery distribution, automobile, and transportation, organizations have implemented information technology between themselves and their business partners in a less aggressive manner, pursuing a strategy of electronic data interchange (EDI) in an effort to get mutual advantage. In most discussions of EDI the focus has been on using information technology to replace paper documents used in routine business transactions. Advocates of EDI point to the potential efficiencies of eliminating the paperwork that is required to support the basic transactions of purchasing or invoicing. They point to the "inherent" logic of extending internal transaction-processing systems beyond the organization's borders to interact directly with trading partners' transaction-processing systems (Figure 3-1). Why print machine-

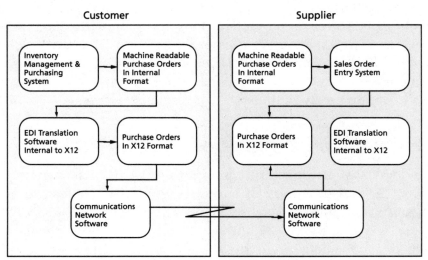

Figure 3.1   *The Logic of Electronic Data Interchange*

readable data onto purchase orders and mail them to suppliers, who will then rekey the data into another automated system?

Regardless of whether individual applications themselves get labeled strategic, the larger trend remains strategically relevant to all organizations—the increased interconnection of information systems across organizations' conventional boundaries. These applications are the barest beginnings of a larger trend toward electronic commerce. While timing is not yet clear, and the details are murky, the endpoint is inevitable.

In a few years, the vast bulk of data flowing between organizations, lubricating the economic system, will be exchanged electronically. Organizations that understand this trend are left with two choices—to wait for the full emergence of the environment of electronic trade, and accept their place in it, or to participate in the shaping of the nature of the new business environment, and define a place that can yield long-term strategic and competitive advantage.

Electronic commerce is paradoxical in that it requires some of the most careful and serious strategic analyses of any current technological phenomena; yet, its success critically depends on how effectively these analyses address the design and implementation of cooperative relationships. The examples of American Airlines and American Hospital Supply provided the evidence for competitive uses of information in strategy design. Efforts to implement EDI center on how to achieve cooperative execution. The current challenge for organizations is to create a new synthesis of *cooperative advantage*.

Each Effort a Piece of the Big Picture

Individual strategic interorganizational systems such as American Airlines or American Hospital Supply do not lead to a transformed business environment. The strategy design perspective that is typically advanced in these examples focuses on the immediate competitive implications of an individual business relationship. Industries pursuing EDI are better attuned to the implications of a new business environment, but they overlook the fundamental need to reengineer business processes in ways that capitalize on new electronic conduits. Each of these perspectives misses important aspects of what individual organizations will need to do to position themselves to take advantage of a business environment that is emerging slowly and erratically today.

The conventional strategic systems perspective applied to interorganizational systems fails by overemphasizing the competitive dimensions of interaction between adjacent organizations in the value chain. The arguments for investing in systems such as American Hospital Supply or American Airlines are advanced to increase customer switching costs, and lock customers in to trading with you. Whether these were part of the actual strategic intent of these systems, or whether they developed over time is questionable and irrelevant. More importantly, as most organizations are now familiar with these tales and the ostensible competitive strategy logic underlying them, trading partners now approach one another warily in considering possible electronic exchanges. Each spends so much time searching for the other's hidden motives that the potential joint benefits of electronic commerce are lost in the shuffle.

Advocates of EDI try to avoid poisoning the trading relationship by promoting industry-level efforts. They frequently do so, however, at the expense of introducing internal changes that can capitalize effectively on the availability of electronic pathways between organizations. In the rhetoric of process innovation, while advocates of EDI may have "replaced the industry-wide cowpaths with superhighways"—they insist on keeping some of the old cowpaths inside the organization, or charging tolls to get on and off the highway. It is an all-too-frequent observation in EDI circles to hear of companies that have implemented an electronic link with a trading partner solely for the purpose of printing out the incoming transmission so that it can be rekeyed into existing transaction-processing systems.

With a little vision, the emerging outlines of a world of electronic commerce become apparent. Any interaction that occurs between companies today—routine ordering, collaborative engineering design, casual correspondence—can be carried out electronically. The fundamental impediment to the dream of the paperless office—getting other offices to stop sending paper—can be eliminated. Moreover, as electronic pathways displace paper as a communications' medium, it will become as straightforward to implement an electronic linkage between systems as it is to set up a telephone conference call today.

Electronic Commerce and Information Strategy

If, in fact, the world is moving towards something that might be called electronic commerce, how should that affect thinking about information and strategy? First, one needs to envision, in its totality, a world of electronic commerce; then, one needs to consider why it is beginning to appear now; finally, one needs to question its implications for strategy.

It takes an immense amount of information to carry out day-to-day interactions between organizations. Much of the first-class mail in the U.S. today consists of purchase orders, invoices, statements, and other business-oriented documents; 1-800 numbers allow individuals to place orders for goods and services with mail-order companies. Fax machines routinely transmit orders and requests for product information.

Suppose you send an electronic mail message to the company librarian requesting a book you've just heard about. The librarian will take this message and call the local bookstore that handles your orders. Someone there will copy down the title and author information, and record an order against your account. Next, the order will get typed or printed onto a purchase order to be sent to the appropriate publisher.

In tracing this simple transaction through the entire chain of organizations that are needed to fill the order, the paper generated in purchase orders—pick lists, packing slips, invoices, shipping labels, phone messages asking why the book still hasn't arrived, etc.—might very well fill the book you've ordered. Within each organization in the chain between you and the publisher, much of the data about the order exists in machine-readable form. At each boundary, however, the data is transcribed and transmitted through some non-automated process, introducing opportunities for errors, misinterpretation, and delay.

Efforts to create EDI in particular industries focus on defining the necessary standards for data to be kept in machine-readable form as it moves between organizations, which eliminates the potential for waste and error that occurs as data is transcribed from one system's format to another.

Staying with the book example for another moment—there is a number on this book (the ISBN) that uniquely identifies both the publisher and the title. ISBNs are designed such that each publisher receives a unique number and assigns numbers to each new title it publishes. Everyone in the industry is now able to identify a particular title using exactly the same ISBN. Thus, the first impediment to keeping data machine-readable throughout the order chain can be eliminated. Once you've looked up the ISBN for a book in *Books in Print*, everyone else along the way can take advantage of your work. No one else need look up the ISBN—everyone knows what title you're talking about.

The Need for Universal Identifiers

So, one precondition for electronic commerce is to find or create some agreed-upon way to identify the objects people are interested in trading. For books, there are ISBNs. In the grocery and retail industries, trade groups have defined the UPC—Universal Product Code. In the market for gemstones, jewelers have created a language to describe the size, cut, and quality of stones, so that they can exchange loose diamonds among themselves while maintaining appropriate control over their valuable inventory.

Other industries have made less progress toward defining the products they exchange precisely or simply enough to support electronic interchange of data. To create an electronic market for cotton, for example, the industry first had to agree on a standard scheme to describe the grade and quality of raw cotton. In the electronic components' industry, there are catalogs whose sole purpose is to identify which manufacturers' part numbers are equivalent. If you want to order a one megabit memory chip for a PC, the actual part number will vary between Texas Instruments and Hitachi. If you are indifferent toward the supplier, you would send a paper purchase order to an electronics' distributor, and simply describe your need in functional terms—i.e., "1 million × 1 bit single in-line memory module for an IBM PC computer"—and then rely on the distributor's sales representative to enter the correct part number for the particular manufacturer's memory chips that are in stock.

If you want to send the same order electronically, there may never be a human sales representative who reads the order before it is filled. But how can you provide a description of the chip you need that is detailed and accurate enough to be read and understood by the automated system filling the order?

Creating Electronic Pathways

There are two prerequisites to establishing electronic commerce. The first is to create electronic connections between organizations. This is essentially complete in the U.S. There are multiple choices for moving data in digital form between any two U.S. organizations: they range from using modems on ordinary phone lines to using private transponders on geosynchronous satellites. Technological advances continue to improve capacity and performance. Value-added network services such as GE Information Services and BT Tymnet help simplify the administrative challenges of setting-up and maintaining network connections among multiple organizations. Western Europe and Japan have comparable telecommunications' environments that lag behind the U.S. only slightly. Political issues regarding the control over information crossing national borders, and bureaucratic inertia on the part of nationalized telecommunication services, are the major drags on rapid innovation in these environments. While developing countries have less well-developed infrastructures, they are catching up very quickly. In some respects, their lack of existing infrastructures may given them an advantage over the developed world, enabling them to capitalize on recent technological advances. From the perspective of enabling electronic commerce, it is now both technically and economically feasible to routinely take machine-readable data in one organization and transmit it electronically to another.

Actually transmitting the raw data between organizations is the easiest part of enabling electronic commerce. True electronic commerce isn't feasible until the second prerequisite is in place. The data stream that flows electronically between organizations must be made understandable. There have to be clear, unambiguous rules for interpreting and acting on the electronic data received. In the U.S., Europe, and Japan, the approach to this part of electronic commerce has been to develop standards describing electronic equivalents to the business forms that convey most routine information between organizations today—e.g., purchase orders, invoices, credit memos, bills of lading, etc.

A typical purchase order has substantial information embedded in its design—quantities, part numbers, shipping and billing addresses are all identified by their placement on the physical form. Creating electronic equivalents to this information content requires substantial, and sometimes tedious, efforts at specifying all of the information content of standard business forms, but with enough detail and precision that computer systems can be programmed to interpret the electronic data stream meaningfully.

In the U.S., this process began in the mid-1970s with the transportation industries. With support from the Department of Commerce, and the ruling from the Justice Department that the efforts would not be construed as violating antitrust laws, the rail and trucking industries created the Transportation Data Coordinating Committee (TDCC). The TDCC defined standard electronic representations of the paper forms used within the industry. Individual railroads and trucking companies could then create information systems that could exchange data with customers and other shippers. Subsequently, the TDCC went on to define industry-level standards in the warehousing industry, and later contributed to standards' definition efforts in the grocery industry. At the same time, there were efforts to create industry data exchange standards in the automotive parts' aftermarket, and the retail pharmacy industry.

Large competitors in several industries also used their market power to impose proprietary data exchange standards on their suppliers. For example, the Big Three auto manufacturers imposed proprietary systems on their suppliers. In the retail industry, K-Mart also implemented a proprietary electronic ordering system with many of its suppliers.

This industry-by-industry and competitor-by-competitor approach created a patchwork of conflicting standards. Few organizations operate in a single industry, leading many to choose between maintaining parallel systems or ignoring electronic commerce altogether. In the early 1980s the American National Standards Institute began efforts to define a single set of standards for electronic data interchange that could be applied across industries. These standards are known as the X12 standards, named after the standards development committee. These efforts have been largely successful in reconciling the conflicts between industry standards. Organizations such as K-Mart and the Big Three auto manufacturers have begun efforts to replace their proprietary systems with the appropriate X12 equivalents.

The problem of conflicting proprietary and industry-level standards has also occurred outside the U.S. The International Standards Organization (ISO) created a standards setting effort equivalent to the ANSI X12 committee in the U.S. These standards, known as EDIFACT (Electronic Data Interchange for Administration, Commerce, and Trade) began development shortly after the X12 efforts began. Recognizing the increasingly global nature of commerce, the X12 and EDIFACT committees have been working closely to ensure that their respective standards efforts are compatible.

People Make Electronic Commerce Run

Creating the rules to describe electronic business documents is only part of the problem in making this part of electronic commerce work. When all is said and done, specifying all of the rules needed to create an electronic analogue of these forms may be tedious, but it is straightforward. It's dangerously easy to underestimate the importance of the people in the routine processes that link organizations. There is still a human information-processing task—interpreting the data in the form, and making sense of it from the organization's perspective—that must be understood and reengineered.

In today's systems, this data-interpretation task is often not visible. Clerical staff and sales representatives quietly verify and complete the information on incoming documents so that the necessary internal process can proceed smoothly. Switching to electronic commerce, without recognizing this essential information-processing dimension, can lead to frequent snags during implementation.

For instance, in its early efforts to implement electronic data interchange, Gillette discovered that it was receiving electronic orders that lacked important data, which was present on paper orders. As with many manufacturers, Gillette offers a variety of promotional discounts and allowances to encourage distributors to purchase its products. Each of these trade promotions affected the price of a particular product. On paper purchase orders, this information was communicated by special price codes placed on each order line item. On paper orders, these codes were entered by Gillette sales representatives when they picked up orders from customers. Customers placing orders electronically showed no interest in or willingness to include these price codes. Customers simply expected to receive the best price available. To determine the correct pricing for electronic orders, Gillettte's order-entry staff had to contact sales representatives in the field who could identify the trade promotions that had been negotiated.

This experience prompted two interesting responses. First, Gillette's MIS staff began to investigate whether expert systems technology might be used to determine the appropriate pricing codes without human intervention. Could knowledge about the customer, product ordered, and current promotional plans be combined to infer the most likely price codes? Much more interestingly, Gillette's sales and marketing executives began to evaluate the effectiveness of their promotional pricing practices. Were these practices achieving their sales and marketing objectives? And, perhaps more importantly, were these objectives being achieved at the expense of incurring other costs within Gillette that would nullify the benefits?

Capturing Informal Information

Still, creating rules about product numbering and standards for electronic equivalents of basic business forms is only part of establishing electronic commerce. Not all interaction between organizations fits into standard forms. There is much informal data—such as letters and phone conversations—that accompanies the structured data contained in standard business forms.

Other important interactions between organizations do not involve business forms. For example, an organization designing a new semiconductor chip may want to send its design to a second company for low-volume fabrication. This interaction requires exchanging design data about the chip in ways that do not fit into the ordinary forms for doing business. But companies will want to keep this data in machine-readable form to minimize mistakes and translation times/costs.

These other forms of communication between organizations might usefully be conducted electronically—e.g, electronic mail to transmit relatively unstructured data, and electronic integration of complex systems such as CAD/CAM to exchange highly complex data in relatively low volumes.

Even if all of these possible interactions were supported electronically, they would not necessarily include all possible interactions between organizations. Choosing new trading partners, or establishing the broad outlines of a business relationship, may always require face-to-face interaction that will exist outside of an electronic commerce environment. Nonetheless, electronic flows of informal memos, purchase orders, invoices, CAD data, and more, will link organizations in the future as ubiquitously as the telephone links commerce today.

Electronic Commerce and Process Innovation

Looking past the implementation challenges, what kind of business world can be envisioned where all routine interactions are mediated electronically? Once data is put into machine-readable form, companies will operate in an interconnected business system in which that data can be moved wherever it is needed, without leaving machine-readable form, and in which it can be manipulated, analyzed, and controlled by automated systems, wherever appropriate or necessary. If organizations are true-to-form, most will simply do what they did when they automated their internal processes—they will speed up the mess. But recent attention to business process innovation, including using technology capabilities to radically rethink and restructure business processes, suggests that some companies can view emerging technology capabilities as opportunities for innovations.

Driven both by dissatisfaction with returns from technology investments, and the success of the quality movement, many companies have begun to question and reexamine their assumptions about the way they do business from day to day. There is an emerging consensus that looking at business activities—whether manufacturing products or providing support services—from the perspective of process flow provides great promise for identifying opportunities to rethink, improve, and streamline those activities. Instead of focusing exclusively on the tasks and activities within the discrete functional departments of sales, manufacturing, distribution, or billing, organizations are looking at dynamic processes, such as order management, that cut across the boundaries of functional departments (Figure 3-2).

The availability of guaranteed connectivity between organizations, coupled with stable standards for exchanging data,

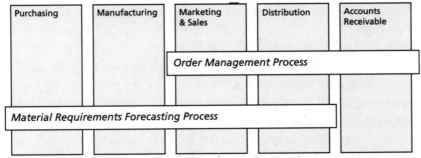

Figure 3.2 *From Functional to a Process Perspective*

makes it possible to imagine all kinds of specific business relationships that could be invented in a world of electronic commerce. But how to manage the transition from today's comfortable and well-understood business processes to this vision of electronic commerce is more problematic.

Moving the data electronically and having standards for interpreting the data as the electronic equivalent of a purchase order isn't enough. The data, however it is transmitted, documents a business agreement between two organizations. This business agreement is negotiated by individuals in each organization, and this negotiation is part of a business process that connects the two organizations in an ongoing relationship. The gradual emergence of electronic commerce suggests that organizations will need to apply a business process reengineering approach to thinking about the processes that link one business to another.

The historical record of the diffusion of technologies, such as the telephone, suggests that the world of electronic commerce is fundamentally inevitable. With the broad outline of such a world at hand, however, it ought to be possible for insightful executives to smooth its arrival and improve their position within it. Certainly, there will be opportunities for new organizations to grow and prosper, providing the services and technology infrastructure that supports a world of electronic commerce. Value-added network companies and auto-

mated clearinghouses will assume new importance in the lu-
brication of the business environment. But companies that
make and sell products and services may also change significantly in a world of electronic commerce. Such a change requires strategic vision and a sense for the organizationally and
technologically possible. The organizing principle that best
captures this vision is contained in the phrase, **implementing
cooperative advantage.** Because it runs counter to the my-
thology of American business practice, it will be difficult to
achieve. However, those organizations that manage to implement the principle are likely to achieve more than their fair
share of competitive advantage, as well.

From Components' Distributor to Inventory Manager

The documents used to support today's business transactions
assume particular business relationships. The availability of
new technology makes it possible to think in terms of new
relationships. Does an organization need to send a purchase
order, electronic or otherwise, to a supplier providing materials on a just-in-time basis? Why not a material requisition?
Perhaps the manufacturer could simply maintain a central database of manufacturing schedules that suppliers would access
directly. Based on knowledge of the manufacturing schedule
and their own manufacturing capacity, suppliers would ship
components to their customers without any formal transaction
at all.

Lex Electronics distributes microprocessors, memory
chips, and other semiconductor components. GE Fanuc man-
ufactures programmable controllers used in factory automa-
tion. In the late 1980s Lex's business with GE Fanuc went
from a few hundred thousand dollars to over six million, over
the course of a single year. This change occurred because GE
Fanuc elected to transfer responsibility for managing compo-

nent inventory to Lex. Rather than simply supply components, Lex was expected to manage GE Fanuc's component requirements to meet GE Fanuc's just-in-time manufacturing schedules. On the surface, this might seem like GE Fanuc simply putting its burden on Lex. In order to make the process work, Lex was given full access to GE Fanuc's material requirements planning (MRP) system. On a technological level, Lex linked its order-entry system with GE Fanuc's MRP system. On the human level, Lex assigned a full-time staff member to work on-site at GE Fanuc, reviewing the interaction between the two companies and the two systems to ensure that GE Fanuc's JIT schedules were met.

Electronic Commerce Forces Internal Process Innovation

Part of the success of process-oriented thinking comes from focusing attention on the customers of a particular process. Curiously, little attention has been given to extending this thinking beyond the individual organization, to electronic commerce.

Process thinking does indeed lead to broader thinking about traditional organizational structures and activities. In the interorganizational context, process thinking calls attention to the continuity of processes across traditional functional boundaries. Instead of thinking in terms of purchasing or sales, process thinking suggests characterizing interaction between organizations as, "managing the resupply process." Just as process thinking can identify duplicate activities across functions *within* an organization, process thinking applied to electronic commerce can suggest opportunities in which to question duplicated activities *between* organizations.

There is a major conceptual leap needed to fully realize the vision of electronic commerce. Organizations must become much more explicit and mindful of the cooperative dimensions

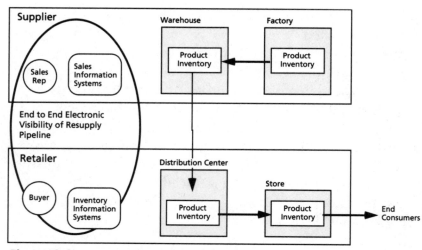

Figure 3.3   *Managing the Resupply Process*

of seeking competitive advantage. The business culture in the U.S. emphasizes the competitive dimension to such an extent that all organizations outside our own are seen as competitors— even customers and suppliers. However, this same culture also obscures how much cooperative behavior must occur to support a competitive environment.

Why is cooperative behavior so critical to enabling electronic commerce? Bringing about electronic commerce is about rethinking the rules of the game. If one team shows up to play water polo while the other comes equipped for ice hockey, it will be difficult to compete, regardless of the talents of individual competitors.

Second Time is the Charm

Consider one early example in the retail industry between a large grocery distributor and a large manufacturer of consumer package goods. In their first attempt at electronic commerce, these two organizations implemented a conventional EDI linkage, where the grocery distributor transmitted electronic purchase orders to its supplier. After a year's pilot test, the effort was abandoned as "uneconomic."

Less than two years later, the same two organizations tried a second time. This time the goal was not "the implementation of EDI." Instead, cross-functional teams from each organization met to rethink and redesign the flow of goods and information between the two organizations. The cooperative goal was to keep the product pipeline full, and at as low a cost as possible to both organizations. Within this context, the question became: how exchanging machine-readable data might support joint management of the logistics pipeline.

In the new design, orders were eliminated as a concept. Instead, the distributor transmits machine-readable data about warehouse shipment levels to its supplier. From this data, the supplier calculates replenishment shipments that will prevent warehouse shelves from running out, but will not unnecessarily increase inventory investment. The result has been a net reduction in inventories of several million dollars, reduction of order cycle times from over twenty, to under ten days, and an increase in fill rates to near 100%. Both the supplier and distributor are now working to extend this logic to their other trading relationships.

In this implementation approach, technology is subordinated to redesigning the basic business process; information is considered in terms of how it can contribute to process improvement goals; and the ultimate benefits depend on cooperative behavior between the two organizations.

The Need for Leadership Buy-In

One of the critical success factors in business process innovation has been obtaining the appropriate level of executive sponsorship and commitment. Integrating processes across business functions within organizations requires support from a high enough level in the managerial hierarchy to balance trade-offs between the functions. Within an organization, making these trade-offs work can be difficult, even though the executives have the explicit charter and authority to mandate a particular solution.

Extending cooperative reasoning beyond the boundaries of the organization is more complex both because there is no explicit structure for resolving trade-offs, and because there are, in many instances, explicit prohibitions against cooperative activities. The first step is acknowledging that cooperative behavior is an issue and that it is an issue requiring executive-level attention. Exchanging even the most routine business document electronically, rather than by paper, raises dozens of policy and procedural issues that are never encountered in the current paper-driven system.

Gillette's experience with price codes is a simple example. In a paper-based world of commerce, the individual processes and information systems of Gillette and its customers are loosely coupled. The sales representatives, buyers, and clerks working in this system have many points at which they can review and interpret data flowing through the system to ensure that both data and product flow smoothly. When Gillette elected to substitute EDI for paper purchase orders, its order-processing systems became much more tightly coupled to the systems of its customers. This tighter coupling means that the who, what, where, and when of decisions must now explicitly and systematically be addressed.

These decisions are not fundamentally technical. Rather, they are decisions about how Gillette intends to do business with its customers. That makes these decisions the responsibility of executives, not systems analysts or computer programmers. Executive decisions about electronic commerce fall into three categories:

- Characterizing the joint business process.

- Selecting trading partners.

■ Allocating costs and benefits between trading partners.

Getting a Jump on Electronic Commerce

What those organizations making progress with electronic commerce have done is to begin characterizing their efforts in terms that capture business process goals more clearly, and subordinate technology details to these business goals. In manufacturing, for example, much progress has been made in accepting, "just in time," as a business process concept that can drive choices of technology. In fashion retailing, the term "quick response" is emerging to describe a particular strategy for cooperative efforts. In consumer products' distribution, "continuous replenishment" is the descriptive term.

What all these terms have in common is an effort to describe a joint business process in terms of business-oriented process goals. This accomplishes two things. First, it engages executive attention by focusing on the business rather than the technological dimension. Second, it provides a shorthand summary of the business goals that can be used in working through implementation trade-offs.

Once an organization has figured out how it wishes to characterize its venture into electronic commerce, the characterization helps determine the trading partners who would be the best involved at each stage of implementation. Viewed as a purely technological phenomenon, organizations implementing electronic linkages tend to focus on safe, pilot-project approaches. They choose peripheral trading partners or small pieces of business with larger, long-term partners.

Chosen by the technological considerations of low-level implementors, these pilot projects are low-risk, but also run the larger business risk of proving inconsequential. Efforts to implement EDI in a number of organizations have stalled in the pilot stages because the implementation efforts were not positioned in meaningful business terms, and the trading partners for the pilot efforts were chosen haphazardly.

Organizations that have characterized their electronic commerce efforts in terms such as "quick response" or "continuous replenishment" have proven much more thoughtful in their choice of appropriate trading partners. As a general rule, trading partners of much greater importance are selected for the initial implementation efforts. This is not to suggest that these implementations are carried out without regard to technical risk, or without the appropriate use of pilot testing and other sound project management techniques. Rather, they are carried out with a much clearer picture of the business objectives to be accomplished.

In the case of the grocery distributor, the continuous replenishment effort was pilot tested with one product category supplied by one of the distributor's largest suppliers. The potential (and subsequently realized) benefits from the pilot test alone were high enough to attract and keep the attention of senior-level executives during implementation. Success during the pilot also established momentum for extending the technology to other product categories and suppliers.

Negotiating Costs and Benefits

The final set of executive decisions in implementing electronic commerce have to do with allocating costs and benefits among the trading partners. This is the area in which cooperative behavior becomes most important. One of the difficulties in successfully applying process thinking *within* organizations is that costs and benefits are not evenly distributed between existing functions of the organization. One part of the organization may have to incur higher costs in the new process to obtain the overall benefits of a reengineered process. Within an organization these tradeoffs can be largely managed by pushing process-innovation decisions higher into the organizational hierarchy (Figure 3-4).

Within a traditional organization hierarchy, there will ultimately be an executive—even if it must be the CEO—who has authority over all the separate organizational pieces of a new process, and who can dictate the revised distribution of costs to attain the desired process-improvement goals. For many projects within organizations, such as implementing an automated sales analysis system to eliminate an existing manual system, the analysis of costs and benefits is generally straightforward. The costs of implementation and operation are identified and compared against the expected benefits (e.g., eliminating clerical positions). Whatever the choice of method, costs and benefits can be compared in order to judge whether or not to proceed.

Projects with strategic relevance can prove more difficult to evaluate. Identifiable costs and benefits can be enumerated and valued. Other costs and benefits, however, can be more difficult to estimate—even to identify. Reducing the analysis of strategic initiatives to a tally of identifiable costs and benefits

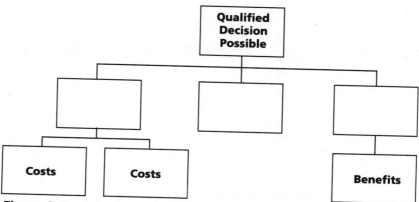

Figure 3.4   *Balancing Costs and Benefits Within the Organization*

may not always be feasible. Nonetheless, organizations make these trade-offs regularly. Although organizations may not do so explicitly, Figure 3-5 suggests one way to model the analysis of implicit trade-offs. Projects, be they new marketing strategies, manufacturing plants, or information systems, have both economic costs and benefits, as well as strategic costs and benefits. Organizations would prefer to implement projects where both the economic and strategic benefits are positive.

In implementing new processes across organizations, there will not be a central authority that can resolve cost/benefit trade-offs spanning separate organizations. The balancing framework suggested in Figure 3-5 is incomplete.

Consider the grocery distributor example again. For the distributor, transmitting data electronically increased order-processing costs. It also increased the average cost per case of product compared to the prior ordering-process strategy of purchasing in bulk quantities when the manufacturer offered promotional discounts. For the manufacturer, there were man-

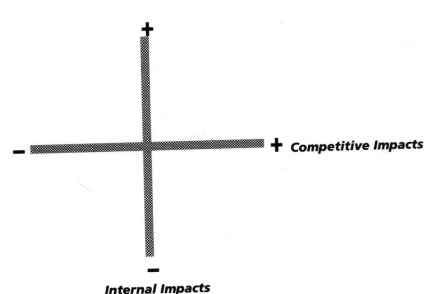

Figure 3.5   *Evaluating Cost/Benefits and Strategic Impacts Simultaneously*

ufacturing and distribution savings if orders were placed more smoothly throughout the year. Finally, there would be the potential joint benefit of reduced inventory investment costs, if buffer stocks for both trading partners could be reduced by streamlining and improving the replenishment process.

Involving the appropriate management levels in each organization made it possible to evaluate the cost-benefit trade-off within each organization. That may not, however, be enough. Presumably, the benefits from implementing a new business process, either in terms of tangible cost savings or improved competitive positioning, must exceed the known costs *for each trading partner.*

Suppose, however, that the call is close for one of the trading partners. This is when the notion of cooperative advantage must be explored. The single-minded analysis suggested in Figure 3-5 needs to be extended to a joint analysis that encompasses both trading partners (Figure 3-6).

In the grocery distributor example, the internal trade-off was marginal, particularly in light of the previously disap-

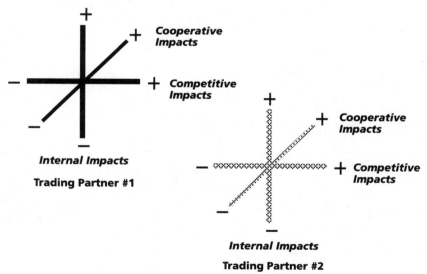

Figure 3.6   *Seeking Cooperative Advantage*

pointing results from the pilot EDI implementation. In this instance, the manufacturer's costs/benefits were clear enough to lead to a cooperative solution. In order to shift the balance more favorably from the distributor's perspective, the manufacturer agreed to supply products under the replenishment program at the average promotional discount offered during the preceding year. This reduced the manufacturer's benefit and increased the distributor's benefit. Now, the cost/benefit analysis for each trading partner was positive. By thinking in terms of the joint system made up of distributor and manufacturer, each individual organization was able to obtain benefits that justified the investment in cooperative logistics processes supported by information technology.

PART III

Strategy

Execution:

Information

Processes,

Architecture,

and Politics

A major challenge discussed in recent research on competitive strategy has been how to translate strategic designs into practical day-to-day execution. Information technology has found its most extensive use in day-to-day operational activities of companies. The chapters in Part II focus on overriding issues about how information can be more effectively managed during execution.

There are many ways that information contributes to more effective execution of company strategies. The use of information and information technology to enable flexible manufacturing strategies is only one example. These uses of information and information technology have been effectively addressed by many other authors. The overriding issues of creating effective information management processes, implementing information architectures, and promoting effective, rather than political, information behaviors have not received adequate attention.

There appears to be a general trend in recent business thinking that emphasizes the importance of process thinking, partly as an effort to redress problems inherent in conventional functional approaches to business. Chapter 4 considers the implications of treating information management as a key cross-functional process in organizations. Functional approaches to information management have dispersed responsibility for information across several discrete functions—information systems, library services, market research, etc. These functions will most likely continue to exist in most organizations into the foreseeable future. The alternative perspective of process asks what can be done to improve the distribution and use of information across functions.

The metaphor of architecture has appealed to information specialists for some time. Success in defining and implementing information architectures has been less forthcoming. Architecture is the study of how different physical spaces contribute to the human activities that take place within those spaces, and is about the processes of helping individuals create spaces to meet their needs. What can be gained by extending the architecture analogy to information? How do different kinds of "information spaces" contribute to meeting the information needs of organizations? What processes need to be followed to help organizations define and create effective information architectures?

Information processes and architectures exist to promote certain kinds of information behavior within organizations. Information doesn't acquire value for the organization until it is put to use. How individuals behave toward information—how they acquire, filter, analyze, and communicate it—is as important to the organization as the information itself. If information is the raw material of decisions, information behavior encompasses the value-creating—and destroying—activities that act on the raw material. What new behaviors do organizations want to encourage with information? What old behaviors become undesirable?

4

Managing Information from a Process Perspective

This discussion of strategy and the role of information within strategy processes would be of little value without discussing how an organization sets about a process for managing information and an approach to developing an information architecture that grows out of the information management process.

A model to describe information management (Figure 4-1) must be generic because: 1) Information receives differing emphases within organizations and within industries. While one can emphasize the importance of information to *any* organization, it is equally clear that information plays a different role within, for example, a pipe manufacturer than within a pharmaceutical firm. While the criticality of information within an organization does not place restrictions on the model, it often highlights and emphasizes the relative importance of the entire process.

2) Differing tasks within the model assume differing levels of importance and value between organizations. For example, the acquisition of new information is vital for many professional service firms that continuously need information on potential clients and business opportunities, and are presented with varied information challenges by new assignments. Using this same model, information classification and storage assumes

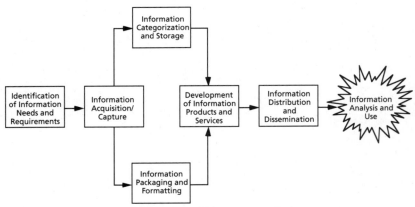

Figure 4.1　*Information Management Process Tasks*

paramount importance in most financial services firms where customer information, records, and other varied documentation must be maintained for both business and regulatory reasons.

Current State of Information Management

While at least 45 periodicals published in the U.S. have "Information" in their titles, and countless conferences, seminars, and programs ostensibly are dedicated to information, the high costs of implementing Information Technology (IT) projects have riveted management's attention on the T in IT, and preempted discussion of issues concerned with information itself.

The heavy emphasis on financial and internally generated data at the expense of non-financial and externally generated information has led, in many instances, to a narrow definition of information. Since early commercial computers were better suited to manipulate numbers than to work with unstructured textual documents, accounting functions were the first automated functions. For a number of reasons, not least of which was the desire of computer vendors to devise new uses for their products, these functions evolved into "Management Information Systems." While it is undeniable that accounting and financial information are an important subset of management information, it is equally true that the idea that accounting systems are really Management Information Systems is as distorting as the identification of Information Technology with Information.[1]

Because of management's failure to focus on information issues, few organizations know what information they have or need. Many managers will exclaim at this point "What do you mean—we spend x millions of dollars to resolve those very issues." But what most IT systems do is try to model the *data* needs of their environments—often a very different matter. In fact, many of the attempts to design discrete data models and enterprise-wide models have been shown by recent research to be unproductive and inefficient.[2] In the ensuing process, information gets short shift.

It is no wonder that the CEO of a major consumer goods' firm told one of the authors, "We continue to spend tens of millions of dollars on information systems, but I never seem to get the information I really need." In addition, there is rarely any single executive within an organization who takes "ownership" of the collection of tasks we call Information Management. There are, of course, Chief Information Officers, who manage the acquisition and maintenance of technology, but they rarely involve themselves, or have a deep understanding of the myriad uses of information. And while some companies, such as Polaroid, IBM, and Merck, have executives who manage information and information processes, it is a relatively rare occurence.

Information Management Roles

As Figure 4-2 shows, most organizations have four major categories of employees who are seriously engaged in at least *some* of the tasks associated with information management. Two of them are considered functionally as "information managers": corporate library staffs and information systems' professionals.

Corporate Library Staff

The staff of corporate libraries, research units, and Information Resource Centers all have a vested interest in promoting the role of external information within an organization, and are

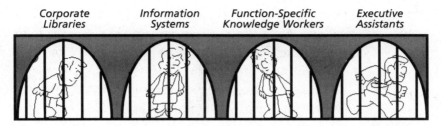

Corporate Libraries	Information Systems	Function-Specific Knowledge Workers	Executive Assistants

Each "cell" focuses on different

- ◆ content
- ◆ format
- ◆ process phase
- ◆ enablers

with little contact between them

Figure 4.2   *Who Does Information Management?*

usually trained in the identification, acquisition, categorization, and storage of externally generated materials, i.e., journals, books, purchased reports, etc. However, librarians rarely interact with the other corporate information players, and, in many ways, their roles are becoming increasingly marginalized.

There are many reasons for this, some related to business pressures. But perhaps the most relevant cause is their failure to take responsibility for their "output." Often they deliver a collection of materials that "seem" to match user requirements, without actually analyzing the information they offer in regard to quality, timeliness, accuracy, relevance, and value. Recently, a study of 164 large corporate libraries[3] found that they were "liked" by employees, who viewed them with "goodwill" because of librarians' eagerness to help and share information. However, their most valued service was shown to be on-line searching of commercial databases—a service that an increasing number of end-users now do for themselves.

Librarians, however, sometimes provide a valuable service that is rarely mentioned in texts on library services. This is the information librarians keep in-house about who in the corporation has looked for similar materials in the recent past. In one consulting assignment, the manager of a large Information

Resource Center for a Fortune 50 firm asked for help in a company-wide quality initiative to determine the most valued services her unit offered patrons. A tentative list cited ten products and services users would rank as valuable. However, users rated an eleventh service *most* useful: to assist them in finding others within the organization who could help with their research.

What would happen is that the user would call a librarian, asking for a literature search on a market, technology, competitor, etc. The librarian would respond: "Did you know that Joe Smith in International is also looking at that issue." In quite a few cases, the patron canceled the request and went off in search of Joe! Neither the consultants nor the Center's management had ever thought to list this service in the survey, since it was not formally acknowledged in the Center's job descriptions, promotional materials, or job evaluations.

This anecdote highlights another point that needs to be emphasized: people prefer to use other people as sources of information, and they need tools to identify the right people to seek in their pursuit of valuable information.

Information Systems Professionals

For certain process tasks, systems' professionals have functional strengths that librarians lack—e.g., development of information products and services, and information distribution and dissemination—tasks for which an in-depth knowledge of technology is essential. The systems' research and methodology literature offers many examples of how to develop information products and services that can bring a true competitive edge to an organization, moving it towards its strategic goals. But these systems' departments are rarely conversant with information content, identification, or acquisition. The point is inescapable: if systems' professionals join forces with the other major information functions, their efforts to deliver strategic products and services will prove to be even more beneficial to the organization.

While the first two groups of information management personnel usually have, (formally or not), the word, "information," in their titles, a large percentage of the real information work done in organizations is done by two other groups of individuals.

Function-Specific Knowledge Workers

Knowledge workers, as defined by the U.S. Commerce Department, now make up a solid majority of the white-collar work force. While the generous definition includes bank tellers, fast-food managers, etc., it also includes accounting and finance professionals; public, investor, and press relations people; business analysts; marketing and market researchers; internal consultants; R & D professionals; planners and strategists; and of course, many general managers.

These employees all work closely with information, usually of a specific type, often qualitative in nature. Where do they get this information? Does anyone outside of the group know what they have, or don't have? Are they served well by the two groups of information professions?

Recent research[4] indicates that knowledge workers usually create their own networks of information providers—both formal and informal—and use that network for all information needs not available "at hand." While they all make varying use of corporate libraries and information systems, few knowledge workers feel that these groups can be relied on for more than a modest amount of their information needs. These individual or group networks are primarily based on other individuals, vendors, and consultants who can "digest" and evaluate written information before forwarding it. When one asks a member of his or her network in the systems' field for a good article on the outlook for UNIX systems, that person doesn't say, "I have hundreds, take your pick." It is much more likely—

especially if the colleague has a commercial relationship—that the person would select an article based on specific needs. The existence of these many informal networks in organizations begs the question: What do you do with them?

Executive Assistants

Executive assistants are non-function-specific knowledge workers. They more often than not work for executives and assist them in such tasks as planning, report writing, and presentation production. It would be a serious error to assume that this group is comprised of bright 25 year-olds marking time before returning for a M.B.A. degree. To the contrary, many are quite senior in title and stature, not unlike senior Congressional staffers, who play such a crucial role in researching, drafting, and passing legislation. It would be hard to estimate how many people perform this role, but the work they do always has a disproportionate effect on an organization's performance.

The non-specific nature of the projects often places even a stronger burden on their information channels. And they often find frustrating the search for information through the organization's traditional functions, for three reasons:

1. Their needs are too diverse, "one-off," and cross-functional for the organization's information systems to be able to respond.

2. Requests are often of the "I need it yesterday"-type, which makes it difficult for a corporate library, whose average Fortune 500 size only includes three or four professionals, to be responsive.

3. The "answers" to their requests are often not structured, in print, easy to obtain, or simple. This makes it particularly difficult for the tools of the library and systems' groups—the printed page and the computer—to help.

Within larger organizations, the informal information network functions smoothly, since the organization's size allows executive assistants to find many of their sources "within the fold." They can also use the clout of those for whom they work to command a timely response.

Formulation of the Information Management Process

With an understanding of the players in the current fragmented state of information management, it becomes possible to formulate a generic information management process.

The word *process* has several differing usages in organizational settings. For these purposes, the term means a set of logically connected tasks that usually cross functional boundaries, and have an owner who is responsible for their ultimate success.[5] As Figure 4-1 shows, the output of this process is determined by work that needs to occur in a coordinated fashion across the traditional "smokestack" functions of information. Employing such a process orientation to information management keeps the strategic value of information in focus.

Information Management Process Tasks

1. Identification of Information Needs and Requirements

In many ways, this is the most important task within the process. Ironically, identification is often taken for granted by systems' designers who act as if they can assume, intuit, or guess the information needs of those they are trying to help. Even in the case of more basic transactional systems, where one might imagine that the information requirements are simple and obvious, there are options that creative information professionals can employ to make systems more strategic, and therefore more valuable.

There are three important points to recognize when undertaking this task:

- **Requisite Variety:** This is a term from biology, used in this context to mean that the number of sources that serve as input to a system need to be as varied as the environment the system seeks to interpret. Simply put, if you are trying to build a unit on your own competitive business environment, you will need as varied a collection of sources as the competitive environment itself. This is why packaged "executive support systems," that have one or two commercial news services as external feeds, fail to live up to their promise of supplying "all" the information an executive could want. The complexity, volatility, speed, and sheer unpredictability of the current business environment mandate that your information needs better be as varied as the factors that go into influencing your organization.

- **People Don't Know What They Don't Know:** Often when interviewing managers to discern their "true" information needs and requirements, the interviewer is faced with either silence or a baffled stare. Respondents can't answer many questions concerning strategic information because they haven't a clue whether such information exists, either within or outside the company; or if it exists, whether it can be obtained, put into a system, or delivered in a timely manner.

  To resolve this issue, information professionals need to be conversant with the available sources of information that could be of value to the client or client organization before doing the interview. In this way, one can bring to the "information needs" interview a much stronger content orientation. In the same fashion, it is remarkably valuable when discussing information needs to show actual examples of how other organizations manage their information, or select models or prototypes of information sources designed by the process team or consultants.

When a librarian or information specialist, who is a content expert, works with a systems' designer, who is an expert in the design of technology systems, they can often produce a requirements plan that is much more "rich" and strategic than anything produced by a single group working alone. While this synergy can work well, the more common case is one in which the technology professional works alone, and is faced with the multi-varied information needs of management, and must relegate "content" to what is implied by the system's technology needs.

- **Information Acquisition/Capture:** Once there is some consensus about the information needed by the clients who will make up the user group, there must be a systematic plan to either acquire the information from its originating source or to capture (electronically or manually) the information from its internal developers.

  This task, too, is far more effectively performed when the content specialists work with systems' professionals. And this task also needs to be performed with considerable creativity. As one successful information consultant has said, "When the user desires the moon, I'd rather say, 'How do you want it represented' than, 'There are no moons available to be configured.' "

  An interesting example of using information that

is rarely captured comes from a large Japanese insurance concern. It had long been the business practice in Japan that after a manager went to a conference, he would have a meeting with peers to discuss what he had learned, whom he had met, what he had heard, etc. When the company was redesigning its management systems, it was decided that these reports were too valuable to be limited to those few people who could attend the one-time debriefing session. The reports were then taped, transcribed, assigned key words for easy on-line retrieval, and mounted on all critical management systems. Thus, anyone on the system could identify a report, and print or read the full text. A life cycle subroutine was also developed to insure that the system was maintained efficiently.

Building a system that will carry information like this involves information skills that go beyond the skills required to build most transaction-based systems. For example, just how *do* you determine the life cycle of each document? Do the same key words work for technicians, executives, and field agents? Because of issues like these, the system was designed by a steering committee with representatives from many different internal functions.

2. Information Categorization and Storage/Information Packaging and Formatting

These two tasks flow out of the previous one and frequently occur simultaneously. They need to be planned as one task, even though they can be understood and analyzed as separate work.

Categorization and storage involves figuring out how users will best be able to retrieve the information they need, and determining the best place to store this information. There are many technical considerations that occur here and are outside the scope of this book. However, a number of important points remain that are often neglected due to this necessary technological emphasis.

- **Make Sure the System is Suited to the Way Users Work with Information.** The best way to do this is to make certain that users help design the system interfaces. The process structure helps guarantee this since the key users of information would be working to build the systems at all task levels.

- **View Information Categorization from Many Angles.** One large consulting firm built an "Experience Center," staffed by eight information professionals, whose mission was to capture, categorize, store, and make available the *experiences* of the consulting staff doing client work. The storage mediums range from cassette tapes and paper transcriptions, to videotapes and CD-ROMs. The categorization scheme is as varied as the nature of the material represented, with indexes available on-line and in-print that allow one to choose material using descriptors such as, style of presentation, methodology, current or potential client, friendly, hostile, or indifferent audience.

- **Do Not Ignore the Design Dimension.** Giving management huge printouts, or access to an extremely large database, without some shortcuts and guides to facilitate a quick response is not an enhancement to management information—it is an impediment.

  We know a prominent researcher on the human Genome project—an endeavor that seeks to map every human gene—who receives between 150 and 200 e-mail messages a day from other researchers and administrators. If he were to read them all and respond only to those he was directly asked to respond to, he would no longer be a scientist; he would be, in effect, a respondent. Yet there is no systems' feature that enables him to effectively screen the messages; a way for him to spend a few seconds determining just what the message contains. Nor is this offered to the senders, who are often in the same position. It wouldn't take much effort to redesign this system to make it more effective; yet, it has not been done because the system administrator thinks that the matter is trivial.

3. Development of Information Products and Services

It is usually this task in which the ultimate system users can make good use of their own knowledge and experiences to bring unique perspectives to the process. Information specialists and system designers and builders are often, and not surprisingly, immersed in the technical arcanae of their disciplines. Knowledge workers must be allowed to contribute to the planning and designing of products and services that they and others will use.

Again, there are several points that bear upon this task and should be heeded.

■   **There is No Such Thing as a "People-less" System.** Oftentimes, the more strategic an information system is, the more human effort is required to maintain it. One of the authors of this book was the project leader for building an Executive Information System for the overseas division of a large American electronics manufacturer. The client executive in charge of the project insisted that "no human hands" were needed to input current international news into his system—that the Nexis database news feed would do fine for all of management's needs in this field, if the system had the correct key words programmed in it. However, Nexis has many publications on-line, and any single important story is often carried by almost all of the leading publications covered by the system. Therefore, all of the executives (about 70) that had access to this system received abstracts from up to 115 news sources on any one significant event. However, if you limit the number of news sources, you decrease the "richness" of the feed. The only practical solution is to employ a human filter for choosing which stories will go on the system.

This contrasts with what the Toshiba Company does.[6] Toshiba has a daily news alert service, which is circulated electronically to over 600 executives. It is produced by a team of four analysts, who continually monitor all international news from wire services, print sources, even television reports. The analysts then choose those stories that are relevant to Toshiba; decisions that are not always self-evident, and that require considerable judgment. After a story has been chosen for distribution, the next step is to review the way the story has been presented by the various media, and compose one version that incorporates the salient points and analyses that will have the most meaning for Toshiba executives. This step also requires both judgment and abstracting skills, especially the sort of intuitive judgment that enables one to seek out the information that would be valued by those who are the system's ultimate customers. By explicitly providing a human dimension to their news abstracting and summarizing service, Toshiba gains additional value because the analysts can adjust and account for biases and special factors (such as the qualifications of the author) in the sources of information that may not be evident in the text itself.

These contrasting examples aren't being cited to emphasize the great work on information that many Japanese firms conduct (some U.S. companies have similar groups), but to point out that, at this stage of technological development, an information system needs some human agents to effectively deliver timely external information.

Another example would be technical support hotlines, which are offered by many computer software producers. When you call Microsoft or Borland with a question, for example, the technical representative frequently has access to a database of trouble reports, indexed by product and problem, from which they can assist you. The representative can access previous answers to questions and find out, "Oh, yes, we've had that happen. Here is the solution." Or the representative can save the question and solution in a new trouble report file to assist the next person who calls. This procedure makes the technical representatives consistently more effective than those of other organizations.

This system can also be used in product enhancement, new product development, and market research, as Shoshana Zuboff writes in *In the Age of the Smart Machine*.[7] The procedure allows for taking data, putting it in a system, and, as a by-product, producing reports on customer complaints for management. This provides management with a much richer view of customer service, and enables them to say, "Look, we are getting a lot of complaints on how this machine works in this environment."

Corporate Yellow Pages

In each of these successful systems there is an element of human interaction that brings much value to the system. However, there are also information products and services that specifically focus on individuals within the organization who, for reasons of organizational design or sheer serendipity, have knowledge that can be very valuable to others in the firm. These people need to be identified, and information products and services need to be successfully built around them. For convenience sake, we have grouped these workers into three categories, as shown in Figure 4-3. However, in practice there is much overlap between the categories, and it is possible for one person to work in all three modes.

Many companies are beginning to use these individuals in ways they have never before been employed. Employee "Yellow Pages" are being produced, which locate individuals by specialties, functional knowledge, even relevant "hobbies." These guides to people are usually more heavily used than guides to written sources.

At one large company, a marketing group decided to publish a general guide to sources of marketing information, including information from syndicated reports, other guides, loose-leaf services, and other information resources the firm subscribed to. This was done with the laudable intent of leveraging these expensive assets to make them more accessible to all.

Experts
- ◆ Function-based knowledge workers who have in-depth knowledge

Filterers
- ◆ Individuals who take in much varied information and filter it for quality, relevance and timeliness

Networkers
- ◆ Human PBXs/information rich employees who create and use informal information networks to distribute information

Figure 4.3   *Information Specialists*

The guide was attractively printed and distributed, and then died a quiet death due to employee indifference. When the guide's producers conducted feedback research they discovered:

1. The materials referred to in the guide were often a year old the day they were printed, and therefore offered limited value to planners.

2. The reports were not where they were cited to be, or were otherwise unattainable.

3. It was difficult to get the individual who "owned" the report to send it to a requester—the fear of permanent loss was substantial.

4. It also wasn't easy to reach the externally generated report's author to question him or her about methodology, sources, definitions, etc.

The guide, in short, was one-dimensional.

This feedback led the marketing team to write a completely new version of the guide, one that listed *employees* who knew about the subjects of the previously listed reports. This version "sold out" and was a great success. Whereas previously, if one wanted to get a sense of where a specific market for a particular technology was going, one had to find a report on the subject, get one's hand on it, and possibly even speak to the author. With the new guide, one could call Jane Smith (listed by her knowledge of the technology) and ask her, "Where's this market going?" Again, this guide was produced by a process team which consisted of users, marketing information specialists, marketing managers, and systems' professionals.

What products like this do is *systematize* informal channels and networks that have always existed in organizations. The difference between the present and the past is that technology has given us the power to put such a system in place,

and management has realized the strategic value of information—including the enormous amounts of valuable information that reside in individuals.

Here is another example of how this process task can bring value. At the advanced technologies' division of an information technology manufacturer, it was well-known that employee Steve Nelson knew all that one could ever want to know about chip manufacturing processes. He even guest-lectured on the subject at a prestigious technical university near his home.

When he was promoted to a more senior management position, he continued to read on the subject, although his job responsibilities substantially changed. However, he still received many inquiries, through the company's many formal and informal channels, based on his reputation as an expert. It took a few years, but the company's senior management finally acknowledged Steve's incredible value and created a position for him, where he spends his time officially doing what he unofficially did before. He is now acknowledged as an information source for the company.

Information Distribution and Dissemination

In working on this task, those professionals who came to the process with a rich and deep understanding of the information needs of key individuals, divisions, or even the entire enterprise, brought substantial value to it. While it is relatively simple to create an information system that is based on predetermined needs, the complexity of the system increases considerably when trying to *anticipate* needs. Yet this is just what many information systems should strive for, if they presume to be strategic in value.

Here are some key lessons we have learned from working on this process.

Be Pro-Active

There are many ways to do this. Some information centers build systematic matrices of information needs by units, or even key individuals. These show clearly *who* is interested in *what* information. The centers then periodically scan the professional literature, through commercial databases, and distribute articles on a pro-active basis, based on the interests illuminated on the matrix. This type of system takes considerable effort, but in those companies where it has been put into place, the users have found it invaluable—often finding important material they never would have otherwise seen.

For more immediate needs, some companies employ their own broadcast network. Several stock brokerage firms have units that scan the key news and market reports early in the morning, and broadcast a short news and alert service to their retail outlets across the country before the brokers make their morning calls.

At the Polaroid Corporation, the Competitive Business Environment group writes a "bulletin" whenever a story breaks that is important to the company. This bulletin is distributed both in paper format and electronically and is often no more than one page. However, it always has a key section: "What this news means to Polaroid." It is interesting to note, in our process context, that Competitive Business Environment is staffed with a marketing executive, a business analyst with an information systems background, and a librarian.

Negotiate with Key Users for Special Services

Occasionally members of an information unit will become aware through observation or through professional reading, of an information need that the organization is not addressing. Since designing and implementing such a system may prove expensive, it is always worthwhile to discuss and negotiate the costs and the value of establishing such a system with those who would most benefit from it.

At a major U.S. diversified manufacturer, much respected for its management practices, the corporate library struck this kind of deal with the R & D division. The library would interview key scientists, engineers, and researchers to determine what classes and categories of research they were doing. The library then set up a dynamic database of these classes, corresponding to the universal patent code. These patent codes were searched monthly through the commercially available world patent database (which even lists patents applied for), and patents that corresponded to the interests of the company's researchers were retrieved and sent to the researchers without them having to ask.

Fill the Intellectual Gap

When a book that is genuinely insightful about, say, organizational effectiveness, is published, who is there to distribute the book throughout the company? What group has this responsibility? How can employees learn the valued insights that the book contains?

There is one particular information unit that buys multiple copies of books by such authors as Peter Senge, Peter Drucker, Michael Porter, Tom Peters, and other important (and accessible!) business thinkers, and circulates numerous reviews and notices of the books throughout the company to encourage readers to borrow them. Another company produces a monthly newsletter (for which it charges!) that contains abstracts of important articles and lengthy reviews of new books. At our office at Ernst & Young's Center for Information Technology and Strategy, we have a Book-of-the-Month lunch, where, on a rotating basis, someone chooses a book to discuss over a two-hour lunch.

This sort of activity will become more common as companies strive to develop their own intellectual capital as the basis of effective competition in the coming years. As Peter Drucker recently stated, it is necessary for companies to "create the resources of knowledge and of people to respond when opportunity knocks."

Notes

1. See Sharon M. McKinnon and William J. Bruns, Jr., *The Information Mosaic* (Boston, MA: Harvard Business School Press, 1992) for a recent analysis of this subject.

2. Goodhue, D.L., L.J. Kirsch, et al. (1992). "Strategic Data Planning: Lessons From the Field." *Management Information Systems Quarterly* (March):11–34.

3. Matarazzo, James M., Laurence Prusak and Michael R. Gauthier, "Valuing Corporate Libraries: A Survey of Senior Managers." (Washington, DC, Special Libraries Association, 1990).

4. Thomas H. Davenport, *Process Innovation: Reengineering Work through Information Technology* (Boston, MA: Harvard Business School Press, 1992); Sharon M. McKinnon and William J. Bruns, Jr., *The Information Mosaic* (Boston, MA: Harvard Business School Press, 1992); and Richard L. Daft and Robert M. Lengel, "Information Richness: A New Approach to Managerial Behavior and Organization Design" in B. Staw (ed.) and L. L. Cummings (ed.) *Research in Organizational Behavior* (Greenwich, CT: JAI Press, 1984):191–233.

5. Thomas H. Davenport and James E. Short, "The New Industrial Engineering: Information Technology and Business Process Redesign," *Sloan Management Review* 31:4 (Summer 1990): 11–27 and Davenport, *Process Innovation*.

6. Prusak and Matarazzo, *Information Management and Japanese Success*.

7. Shoshana Zuboff, *In the Age of the Smart Machine: The Future of Work and Power* (Oxford: Heinemann Professional Publishing, 1988).

5

Creating an Information Architecture

Information architecture is a term that has been used by various groups within the information systems' community since the early 1980s. It was used as a metaphor by system designers and theorists to denote an enterprise-wide model for data creation and movement. This model, and the methodologies that underlie it, tried to systematically document all the enterprise's relevant data entities (e.g., customers, products, employees, etc.) and data relationships. The ultimate goal was to have a comprehensive "map" of the organization's data, and then to build information systems "based" on this map.

However, these efforts often fell far short of their goals. The most serious drawback of this approach is its assumption that all, or even a majority, of the key information in an organization is structured and formatted to be machine-readable. This is clearly not the case; in most organizations no more than 10% of its information is machine-readable. The 90% of the organization's information that resides outside of automated information systems includes the information contained in paper files and in the minds of its key executives and employees.

Another reason for the lack of success with this detailed data-modeling approach is that when the effort focuses on data elements and data entities, the product is often too granular to hold the attention of the very managers who could benefit most from an explicit and shared information model of the organization and its activities. Without such a model, data only infrequently becomes transformed into usable information.

The current state of practice within the information systems' community is known as "information engineering." Information engineering practice developed in response to problems caused by the proliferation of automated information systems within organizations. As organizations built automated systems to meet specific business needs, they created a patchwork of redundant and inconsistent databases focused on the immediate needs of one particular business function or process, without regard to other functions or processes. This accounts for the emphasis on machine-readable data and detailed data modeling. Even when well done, these approaches create data models that are far too large and cumbersome to be of much practical value to a line manager. One critic recently pointed out that in not so unusual a case "cross relating 200 entities with 130 activities produced a matrix of 26,000 cells. Each must be examined to determine whether the activity creates, reads, updates, or deletes the entity."[1] Clearly, the costs and effort associated with an endeavor such as this is not at all commensurate with any value the model will bring to the business.

Yet, however poorly information architecture efforts have been performed in the past, it is too important a topic to be allowed to languish as a technical exercise. If used to articulate a richer, fuller, and more meaningful picture of information, it can be an essential tool for exploiting information strategically. The following observation from one of the better texts on information modeling articulates the underlying rationale for an *explicitly* developed information architecture:

> The fact these separate vocabularies [i.e., specialized terminologies in different components of the organization] and, more significantly, their implied *separate conceptual frameworks* exist in an organization should be taken seriously: One has to assume that the subject matter is sufficiently complex that a single vocabulary could not arise through normal informal processes. As a result, real intellectual effort is required for investigating and resolving possible differences. Until this is done, any attempt at stating system requirements is bound to be troubled, since no one can be certain exactly what vocabulary has been used in the requirements statement.[2]

As Benjamin and Blunt wrote in the *Sloan Management Review* (Summer 1992), "Without an understandable information architecture, information technology will be unable to bridge the gulf between the new technologies and the business's strategic directions."[3]

The Concept of an Organization's Information Architecture

"Information architecture" is an unfortunate term in so far as it combines two words, both of which have a wide range of connotations. While richly evocative as a metaphor, it increases the challenge of developing a shared definition of key concepts. Even without an established definition, recent surveys have shown that senior information systems executives are seriously concerned with the issue of information architecture. In fact, these executives indicate that information architecture is often their leading issue. But are other senior executives as interested in this issue? Probably not, under its current name; although senior executives are very interested in getting the right information they need to manage their organizations. Arriving at a common definition of what an information architecture really is, and what its potential value is, will go a long way towards providing a bridge between these two groups.

Webster's offers two definitions of the term "architecture" that are relevant here. The first defines it as a "formation or construction as or as if as the result of conscious act," and the second defines it as "a unifying or coherent form or structure."

Management theorists have been talking about the importance and dominance of information in organizations for some time now. Appending the term "architecture" suggests that there is additional value to making the structure and relationships in this information explicit. The creation of a well-defined, commonly agreed-upon, and coherently managed information architecture allows for all parties in a company to speak the same language and to use information to make meaningful decisions.

Information architecture needs to be more than just information engineering in the same way that architecture is more than just mechanical engineering. Engineering is about *realizing* visions within the confines of practical constraints of time, space, budget, and the state of the technologically possible. Architecture is about *articulating* visions that integrate the desires and constraints of clients within the bounds of engineering possibility. Among other things an architect is concerned with the context, environment, aesthetics, regulatory constraints, ergonomics, materials, and models that guide the conscious design of a structure.

The practice and products of the field of architecture provide guidance toward how information architecture can meet the broader strategic needs of organizations:

- The language and practice of architecture have evolved to a point where practitioners can systematically create physical spaces that enhance the human activities they are designed to accommodate. Both a chapel and a lecture hall bring large numbers of people together—but the experiences they evoke are very different. Each can be assembled from comparable raw materials, yet the end results are demonstrably different. The language of architecture makes it possible to talk about these differences without reference to the underlying materials or engineering details.

  In information architecture, on the other hand, discussions of information space often rapidly degenerate into technical considerations. This is principally the result of having no language or tools for carrying out discussions at a suitable client-centered level.

- Physical architecture imposes structure and order on physical space, and shapes the behavior of its occupants. Windows let in light, air, and views. Doors and passages direct the flow of movement and activity. The layout and content of rooms constrain the number of people who can gather and the activities they can conduct.

By contrast, we do not yet have a good understanding of how information architectures shape behavior.

■   In physical architecture, three elements interact in the realization of a particular architectural structure. The physical environment determines the extremes to guard against. Human senses and capabilities create guidelines and establish predispositions that architects can exploit. Evolving building and structural technologies introduce new options for spanning spaces or shielding activities.

By analogy, information architectures should involve corresponding elements for creating information spaces that are conducive to specific activities.

There is an external information environment that exists independently of any single organization or individual. Industries, for example, share common vocabularies and jargons based on underlying manufacturing technolgies. Humans have limits and capabilities for processing information, just as they have limits in their ability to tolerate heat or cold. For example, humans have very limited short-term memories, especially for arbitrary data, yet are immensely effective at recognizing subtle patterns. Finally, technologies continually change the state of the possible reconciliation between human capabilities and environmental realities. As videoconferencing becomes technically and economically feasible, it will no longer be necessary to bring individuals together to obtain the benefits of face-to-face interaction. Figure 5-1 elaborates the analogies between physical and information space by identifying examples in each element—environment, human capabilities, and technology limits.

Element	Physical Space	Information Space
Environment	Local weather profile; temperature extremes and averages; rainfall; winds	Availability and quality of external data
	Terrain; hills and valleys; views worth exploiting/ avoiding	Universe of competitors and their activities
	Soil; stability of foundations; hidden flaws	Current knowledge about the global political and economic spheres
		Knowledge about developing technologies
Human Capabilities	Tolerance for environmental extremes	Short-term memory limits
	Visual and auditory strengths and limits	Information processing and decision-making styles
	Cultural biases and limits on personal space boundaries	Long-term memory strengths and pattern matching skills
Technology Limits	Arch, flying buttresses	Database technology
	Reinforced concrete	Communication networks
	Geodesic structures	Group support technologies
	Materials strength	

Figure 5.1   *Analogies Between Physical and Information Spaces*

Two Audiences for Architecture

The final product of an architecture (be it physical or information) is a structure that uses available technologies to shape and constrain the environment so that a specified set of human activities can be more effectively carried out. While the final structure is the implementation of particular technologies, there are two classes of intermediate design products that must be created to guide the translation from architectural vision to concrete technology. These design products aid the communication process between the architect and the architect's two primary audiences—client and technical specialists. The first class of design products describes and elaborates the architectural vision in client-centered terms. The second articulates the details of the architectural vision for the technical specialists who will be charged with implementation. Figure 5-2 compares these products for physical and information architectures.

In the physical architecture arena these design products and communication tools are well-balanced between client and specialist. Each audience has tools and techniques appropriate to its needs and background. Given its origins in technical practice, the current practice of information architecture is

	Physical Space	*Information Space*
Client-Centered Products	Site master plan Artist's sketches & renderings Scale models Budgets Implementation calendar	Principles of information management Budgets Implementation calendar
Technical Specialist-Centered Products	Blueprints Project PERT/CPM charts Material requirements lists Soil analyses Environmental impact statements	Normalized entity relationship diagrams and data model Data dictionaries and database management designs Data structure diagrams

Figure 5.2 *Key Products Required to Describe an Architecture*

significantly weak in offering client-centered products. This presents a central challenge to creating effective information architectures.

Adapting available technical tools to serve client-centered needs is fraught with risk. Technical tools presume communication between technical specialists who share professional vocabularies and mental models. They are either a shorthand for speeding up information interchange, or tools for articulating technical trade-offs in sufficient detail to drive implementation. Client-centered tools serve an entirely different purpose. They are primarily used to assist nontechnical specialists, who potentially have radically different levels of sophistication, with the articulation of their requirements in enough detail to meet two objectives:

- Provide a basis for the architect to identify the necessary specifications of client requirements that technical specialists will use to carry out their particular tasks.

- Provide a basis for architect and client to communicate and resolve necessary trade-offs and compromises between client desires and the state-of-the-possible.

The architect is the only individual with the requisite training and background to judge whether the translation is accurate. Generally speaking, the gap between client requirements and technical realization is too large to be spanned in a single step. The role of architect emerges to bridge this gap. Creating tools in information architecture to bridge the gap between client and technical specialist requires turning away from technical perspectives in consideration of the client's information architecture issues. This can best be done by considering the goals that a client hopes to realize from an information architecture.

Goals of an Information Architecture

Figure 5-3 suggests the kinds of client-oriented goals that an information architecture should address. In essence, these goals focus on creating an information space that promotes information behaviors that the client believes will help realize broader organizational goals.

An information architecture articulates what information is most important to the organization. It becomes the information component of a strategic vision or an information vision.

Organizations collect, use, and store enormous amounts of information. One of the great benefits of the information age is the ability for decision makers to access and analyze vast data stores from their desktops. In the face of proliferating

---

- Define the information space of the organization in terms of key information domains of interest and key pathways of information flow.

- Define the critical boundaries of the organization's information space (what is inside and what is outside).

- Identify strategies for effective information sourcing, filtering, and reduction.

- Eliminate information noise.

- Make desired information behaviors easier.

- Make undesired information behaviors difficult.

- Improve adaptability by explicitly articulating information assumptions and policies.

- Improve managerial communications by explicitly articulating shared information models.

Figure 5.3   *Goals of an Information Architecture*

sources and volumes of potentially useful data and proliferating technology choices for storing and manipulating this data, most organizations seek to expand their information universe. Very few have thought about the potential value of limiting their information universe.

Although limiting information choices appears contrary to conventional rhetoric, individuals and organizations inevitably limit their own information universe. There are far more signals in the environment than any person or organization can possibly track. The value of being explicit about information choices via information architecture lies in being very conscious of what is being excluded, as well as what is being included.

The essence of strategy is to make difficult choices about what is possible, and to artfully create new opportunities from limited resources. A lazy definition of information architecture calls for providing users with any information at any time. The challenge lies in limiting this utopian request without simultaneously limiting the effectiveness of the organization.

Perhaps it is useful here to describe what an information architecture is not. Although defining a concept this way may seem negative, information architecture, as a concept, is so muddled that any elaboration on its meaning should be welcomed.

- *Information Architecture Is Not A Technology Infrastructure*   There are many ways, methods, and frameworks that define the configuration of hardware, software, people, and policies that make up a technical systems' infrastructure. Architecture is the wrong metaphor to use in defining them.

- *Information Architecture Is Not Data Modeling*   Information is a far more capacious, subtle, and complex realm than data.

- *Information Architecture Is Not Information Systems*

Architecture   This subject, too, has its own body of knowledge that is clearly distinct from any approach to information management. Information systems architecture is a much more technical exercise, more analogous to the working of a renderer or a contractor than to an architect.

Limits of the Architecture Metaphor

Although the architecture metaphor yields many insights, it also suffers from severe limitations. Are there extensions or alternatives to the metaphor that can meet these limits, even as organizations continue to elaborate it?

The two most critical limitations of the architecture metaphor are tightly interrelated. First, it has a bias toward creating new structures. Second, it has a bias toward focusing on the internal environment. Left unaddressed, these biases will lead to architectures that either cannot be implemented or are fatally narrow in their perspective.

In physical architecture, master plans, artists drawings, and scale models tend to ignore the gritty reality of the surrounding environment. Most information architectures have been similarly unrealistic. In the information environment, however, essentially all architectural work is *renovation* work. Much of the discussion of the constraints of prior information decisions (the villages and shantytowns created in the pressure to get critical applications up and running) laments the "problem of legacy systems." From an architectural perspective these past decisions contribute to the information environment within which new structures must operate.

The impact of these legacies depends both on the quality of the structures now in place and on the scope of new opportunities. The bias of current strategic data planning efforts is on creating entirely new information structures to replace the old.[4] Although razing the slums may be appealing on the grounds of architectural purity, practical constraints suggest that careful renovation and restoration may be more appropriate.

The inwardly focused bias of the architecture metaphor is more serious in the competitive economic environment of the 1990s. While an architectural perspective compensates for the information engineering bias on machine-readable data, which excludes equally or more important sources of data; such a perspective still walls off attention to the external environment. This bias is troubling because the complexity, and more important, the volatility of the external environment demands a more dynamic, even organic, perspective.

An architectural perspective tends to encourage efforts to impose order on the information environment to conform to an architectural vision. In a volatile environment it is at best problematic whether any rigidly imposed structure will stand. One of the greatest failings of current information systems is poor adaptability. Architectural metaphors perpetuate a search for stability that may not be achievable. The particular balance between stability and adaptability may be difficult to specify in advance. Perhaps other metaphors might offer better insights toward improving the adaptability of information systems to an environment of steady change.

Another View of Information Architecture

While these impediments to the success of information architecture as a concept are serious, there is still much that can be gained from an expanded version of the major components of information architecture.

Clearly, an organization's information architecture needs

to be influenced by its specific requirements for information integration. Some more centralized companies will have a great need for and will receive much benefit from tightly integrated systems. On the other hand, a large company with relatively autonomous business units may have little need for a high degree of integration. The fundmental concept of an information architecture, however, is applicable to any size organization where people work with information. Robert Waller offers a succint rationale worth noting:

> When humans confront complexity, they must discover these relationships and (in organizatonal life) communicate them to one another in intelligible form. Conscious manipulation of elements and relationships, however, is a function of the short-term memory. As was noted earlier, this part of the human cognitive appartus suffers from some severe limitations.
>
> This comes down to a design problem. . . . Somehow, then, a way must be found that recognizes the central features of complexity and yet takes into account both the strengths and weaknesses of human cognition . . . .
>
> Since neither the human capacity nor complexity can be changed, a way must be found to link the two without changing either. In engineering terminology, an interface device must be sought that will link humans and complexity, while preserving the original properties of each.[5]

This interface is another way of describing information architecture.

Is the value of an information architecture limited to information systems planning? Probably not. Let's take a step back and consider what can be learned simply by thinking about the juxtaposition of the two words, information and architecture. The correct definition of information has been argued endlessly, but a good definition is one that defines information broadly and encompasses data, knowledge, news, and intelligence in a variety of structures and media. Architecture refers to coherent structure. Architecture also refers to a profession and, by implication, to the process by which structure is developed.

During the course of designing a structure architects think about how a group of people will interact with the space around them. On a behavioral level architects think about how space should be allocated, subdivided, and arranged to improve the interaction of the inhabitants. On a technological level they think about how the underlying subsystems of a building (e.g., plumbing, heating, electrical) must fit together with one another and with the public spaces. Architecture combines art and technology to create a usable environment.

In much the same way, an information architect needs to combine art and technology in defining an organization's information environment. The information architect must strike a balance between the organization's information needs and technology limitations. The architect must look to the business strategy to decide what information is important to the organization. In this way, an information architecture can also become the mode of communicating to everyone in the organization what information is important. It can provide a statement on how the organization views the world.

Thinking about information architecture from a process perspective also lets one think about developing information architecture in an incremental, evolutionary way. Conventional information systems (IS) approaches to information architecture focus on the end product of a fully articulated information architecture. When architects and their clients interact, however, there may be many intermediate outputs and models on the way to the final structure. These models serve two purposes. First, they allow the client to visualize the final structure in ways he or she can understand more directly than the specialized notations of architects. Second, they sustain the interest and commitment of the client during the construction of the final structure. Information architects need to think about how they might sustain their client relationships throughout the process.

Information architects need to think about ways of presenting their efforts in ways that match the function of the artists' renderings and scale models of a conventional architect. The modeling techniques used by information architects today are specialized notations for carrying out their own work and communicating with other specialists. They don't have models (beyond prototypes of screens or reports) that convey the essentials of an information architecture to the paying clients—executives.

It is clear that traditional information systems modeling approaches are not sufficient for modeling the true complexity and richness of an organization's information environment. There is no science for metaphor construction that would enable representation of an organization's information requirements in a way that would be understandable and usable by all.

One concept that may hold some promise to this end is the "document." A document in this context is not necessarily paper. A document is any bounded representation of information; it is media independent. A recent Ernst & Young study found that the document is the most useful way to represent information requirements in process-innovation initiatives. These projects focus on achieving breakthrough improvement in business processes. Business processes are defined at a fairly high level in an organization in order to achieve dramatic change. In analyzing these business processes, business managers and others found it easier to articulate requirements when considering documents rather than data elements.

Any approach to information architecture must accommodate the different types of information that business managers and knowledge workers need on a regular basis. Currently this information can be found in databases, documents, and published materials. It exists both inside and outside an organization. It may take almost any form—paper, electronic, phone conversation, etc. An effective information architecture will represent all these types of information and be flexible enough to encompass those that have yet to be discovered.

Alternative Metaphors

There are two other metaphorical schemes that can either replace or supplement the architecture metaphor: language and ecology. While at first sight these choices may seem even odder than "architecture" for describing information systems, they, too, create new ways of thinking about information and its management.

Language

It is vital for any organization to have agreed-upon terms and meanings. In one Fortune 500 company, the CEO went so far as to appoint senior-level executives as "Information Czars" who would develop and determine what constitutes a "sale," "profit," or even a "customer" for each of the company's divisions. This may sound simplistic, but in reality it is a root issue for anyone attempting to build an information system. Often, the system designers accept terms, "as is," neglecting the consensus-building and negotiation that needs to occur before a common language can be agreed upon. As Professor Robert Eccles of the Harvard Business School writes: "Management needs to articulate a new corporate grammar and define its own special vocabulary—the basic terms that will need to be common and relatively invariant across all the company's businesses. Some of these terms (like sales and costs) will be familiar. Others, however, will reflect new strategic priorities and ways to think about measuring performance."[6]

Language here defined also includes the common use of metaphors, symbols, and classifications of information. By establishing common metaphors, an organization can seek control over the ways employees think and perceive the reality of the organization. Even simple slogans, like "Quality is First," or "The Customer is King" are metaphorical, and as such, are interpreted subjectively by employees. How many companies clearly define just what "Quality" or "King" means in these contexts?

By seeking common definitions, systems planners can build systems that can measure an organization's performance as defined by these very concepts. It is an exercise in rhetoric to promulgate terms and metaphors throughout an organization without having a way to measure and capture information about the ways in which these terms and metaphors are being implemented.

Clearly, the use of information as a strategic resource will involve a new vocabulary. The term *information* itself may undergo redesign of its contextual meaning. Categories of information are yet a third way in which language can be crucial, providing legitimization and authority to what is truly important within the realms of information.

To determine, for example, what information is strategic, and will be presented to the management committee, versus what information is not is a serious act, and constitutes a key element of building an information architecture. The executive who managed the agenda (and provided the needed information) for the monthly executive meetings of a Fortune 500 company, when asked what constituted strategic information, replied "What I choose to distribute and what the members bring to the meeting, *de facto*, is strategic." Time spent focusing on information architecture might make this committee more effective, and might inform others in the company about what "strategic" actually means as a category of information.

It is important to stress here how the use of a metaphor can seriously affect how information is perceived. As one recent study points out, "the common metaphor of the 'flow' of information through an organization as if it were some kind of mystical fluid, a life-blood, is totally misleading. It is also damaging because, by describing an information system as a plumbing system, the easiest next step is the introduction of a mechanism to improve the circulation of this fluid. That mechanism invariably is a computer system whether appropriate or not."[7]

Grammar is the set of rules based on usage and prescription which gives language its contextual feel and makes it uniformly understandable. If one considers the elements of an information architecture "language entities," then the grammar sets up the policies, practices, and processes of how the information pieces—documents, images, data-sets, or videotapes—are generated and distributed, and establishes the rules for sharing the information.

The grammar of an information architecture establishes and represents the flows of information in ways that can add value for the user. It can signal those units or even senior individuals who should be receiving information but are not, and vice versa. It provides a map of understanding how information actually *works* to enhance organizational effectiveness. As often as not, merely focusing attention on this issue brings substantial value to the organization.

Grammar includes the sets of rules, process, and procedures that give contextual meaning to the entities of language. By documenting these often elusive and informal acts, one begins to see how an architecture can bring exceptional value to a system design. In addition, by including individuals (experts, filters, networkers) in the official grammar, credence and authority are given to what is already a very valuable information channel.

Ecology

A second approach would be to investigate an ecological approach to managing the information environment. Ecological perspectives have the advantage of already embodying a systems perspective on managing complexity. They have the further advantage of placing great emphasis on the role of the external information environment. From this perspective information ecologists would seek to identify and exploit existing features in the broad organizational terrain. Are there features of the information landscape that can be effectively exploited? What kinds of information structures could be built to fit most naturally into the terrain? Are there natural information springs and streams that can be put to use where they are or be redirected by building dams and artificial lakes?

Traditionally, the models of information and data that have been designed as the templates of technical systems have been hermetic—enclosed by the boundaries of what computer systems could actually manipulate, and by the imaginations of systems designers who were also bounded by technical constraints. Now that these technical constraints are all but gone, and end-users of systems are having a much greater say in what goes into them, it is clear that any information architecture worth pursuing needs to: 1) incorporate more externally generated material into the architectural structure, and 2) create an architecture that is flexible and dynamic enough to incorporate and discard information sources quickly and efficiently.

Some examples come immediately to mind when discussing environmental information that belongs in any architecture. These are listed along with the likely places where such information usually enters the organization:

Environmental Information	Internal Source
Competitive Information	Competitive Information Centers Strategy Departments Purchasing Departments Marketing Departments
Emerging Technologies	Corporate Technology Departments Data Processing/M.I.S. Patent Departments/R & D

Regulatory Issues and Environmental	Legal Departments Investor Relations Internal and External Auditors Human Resources
Global Issues	Strategy Executive Offices
Domestic Policy	Government Relations Senior Management
Demographic and Social Information	Marketing Departments Human Resources/Planning
Customer Information	Marketing EDI/Systems Sales

To give one a sense of how meager current methods are, ask yourselves how many of these information categories exist in your own de facto information architectures. And these categories are by no means inclusive of all critical environmental information. An ecological metaphor, or perspective, ensures that a continuous focus will remain on the relationship between a system and its environment. This focus needs to be as dynamic as the environment itself, and it needs to be adaptable so that it can change as the boundaries shift between an organization and its trading partners and stakeholders.

Examples

An informative, successful attempt to develop a type of information architecture as well as communication system was developed by EPRI, the Electric Power Research Institute, which acts as an R & D consortium for electric utility companies. EPRINET was developed to face "one of the major challenges of the 1990's—how to leverage its huge wealth of knowledge."[8] This system gives access to the digital equivalent of

2.7 million pages of worldwide research reports, report summaries, and other documentation. It has software and document products, access to experts throughout the industry, a sophisticated e-mail component, and expert system-based products.

It is relevant to note here that several of the "critical success factors" that went into the design and building of the system are similar to the points about information architecture we have been making. These factors include:

- Establishing the "right" mix of product offerings.

- Distilling the mountains of information into practical packages such as report summaries, R & D project status reports, and news of hot topics.

- Maintaining the perspectives of the several market segments (executives, planners, research engineers, and operations people) served by the system.

By adhering to these principles, similar to those just discussed, EPRINET has been judged a considerable success by its user groups.

Another innovative use of an information architecture is the MARON Information Network created by the giant Mitsubishi group in Japan. This is a highly decentralized network of information about the internal and external reports various units of Mitsubishi possess. The system was created and is maintained by a group consisting of librarians, systems designers and analysts, as well as subject experts. The most important criterion for keeping material on this network is a wide-angled understanding—almost intuitive in nature—of the users' information needs. This understanding is accomplished by a continual series of interviews, conducted by the systems' designers. Key information acquirers, provisioners, and users determine new or modified information needs that would cause changes in the architecture. This knowledge, in turn, leads to the resolution of the following questions, which are always present when constructing a system around architectural principles:

- What should the strategic thrust of the network be?

- What factors and values should determine what information should go in the network and how is it organized?

- What should the life cycle of a document be?

- What indexing and classification schemes would be most effective?

- What feedback from users is desirable and who should determine system modifications?

However, the most important points to stress are that Mitsubishi overtly acknowledges information as indispensable to the running of its diverse businesses, and that much of the time spent planning and building the MARON Network was allocated toward resolving issues about the design of an information architecture.

The last two chapters focused on the creation and understanding of information processes and architectures. While these two subjects are complex, they are critically relevant, but they have suffered from a lack of attention on the part of management and lack of serious research on the part of scholars. This is even more true of the third element of the relationship between information and strategy execution—information behavior.

The next chapter focuses on the ways individuals and organizations behave toward and with information. We have chosen a political classification scheme to help articulate and analyze these behaviors, since politics is the art that decides who gets what, when, and how.

Notes

1. Tony Bidgood and Bob Jelley, "Modeling Corporate Information Needs: Fresh Approaches to the Information Architecture," *Journal of Strategic Information Systems* 1:1 (Dec. 1991).

2. Sally Shlaer and Stephen J. Mellor, *Object-Oriented Systems Analysis: Modeling the World in Data* (Englewood Cliffs: Prentice–Hall, 1988).

3. Robert Benjamin and Jon Blunt, "Critical IT Issues: The Next Ten Years," *Sloan Management Review* 33:4 (Summer 1992):18.

4. Dale Goodhue, Laurie Kirsch, Judith Quillard, and Michael Wybo, "Strategic Data Planning: Lessons From the Field," *MIS Quarterly* 16:1 (March 1992):11–34.

5. Vincent P. Barabba and Gerald Zaltman, as cited in *Hearing the Voice of the Market: Competitive Advantage Through Creative Use of Marketing Information*, (Boston: Harvard Business School Press, 1991):49.

6. Robert Eccles, "The Performance Measurement Manifesto," *Harvard Business Review* (Jan.–Feb. 1991):131–137.

7. Jonathan Liebanan and James Backhouse, *Understanding Information*. (London: Macmillan, 1990):119.

8. Marina Mann, Richard L. Rudman, Thomas A. Jenckes, and Barbara McNurlin, "EPRINET: Leveraging Knowledge in the Electric Utility Industry," *MIS Quarterly* 15:3 (Sep. 1991):403–421.

6

The Politics of
Information[1]

In a *Harvard Business Review* article a shoe company executive wrote: "On one of my first days on the job, I asked for a copy of every report used in management. The next day, 23 of them appeared on my desk. I didn't understand them . . . Each area's reports were Greek to the other areas, and all of them were Greek to me."[2] He might have more accurately described these reports as coming from Athens, Sparta, Corinth, Thebes, and Peleponnesia—each part of the organization a separate political domain, with its own culture, leaders, even vocabulary.

In looking at information management approaches in more than 25 companies over the past two years, it has become clear that most have failed, or are on the path to failure. The primary reason for this failure is that the companies did not manage the politics of information. Either information management initiatives that were inappropriate for the overall political culture were proposed, or when politics were encountered in an information initiative, they were treated as peripheral rather than integral to these initiatives. Only when the politics of information are consciously managed and viewed as a natural aspect of organizational life will true information-based organizations emerge.

Furthermore, there is increasing logic and evidence behind the assertion that as information becomes the basis for organizational structure and function, politics will increasingly come into play. The most information-oriented companies are least likely to share that information freely. As people's jobs and roles in companies become based on the unique information they hold, they may be even less likely to share that information—viewing it as a source of power and uniqueness. When information is the primary unit of organizational currency, owners will not give it away.[3]

When owners of key information resist sharing it either outright or, more commonly, through bureaucratic maneuvers, they are often dismissed as being unfair or opportunistic. Yet there may be quite legitimate reasons for withholding the information.

Models of Information Politics

The 25 companies studied enable the identification of five information models—or, to continue the political metaphor, "states" (Figures 6-1 and 6-2). Three of these—technocratic utopianism,[4] anarchy, and feudalism—are less effective than the other two, monarchy and federalism.

In any given organization there may be proponents for more than one of these models. Sometimes they are in conflict; sometimes one predominates. Making these models explicit and then choosing a single desired state is one way of managing information in a more effective and realistic way. Maintaining multiple models is confusing to the organization, and consumes scarce resources. Once a model has been selected, an orga-

Technocractic Utopianism	A heavily technical approach to information management which stresses categorization and modeling of an organization's full information assets, with heavy reliance on emerging technologies.
Anarchy	The absence of any overall information management policy, which leaves individuals to obtain and manage their own information.
Feudalism	The management of information by individual business units or functions, which define their own information needs and report only limited information to the overall corporation.
Monarchy	Definition of information categories and reporting structures by the leaders of a firm, who may or may not willingly share the information after collecting it.
Federalism	An approach to information management which is based on consensus and negotiation of the key information elements and reporting structures for the organization.

Figure 6.1   *Models of Information Politics*

Company	Federalism	Monarchy	Tech Utop	Anarchy	Feudalism
Office Products	X		X		
Software		X		X	
Medical Supplies			X		
Computers	X			X	X
Consumer Goods			X		X
Electronics					X
Consumer Goods					X
Chemicals			X		X
Info. Services			X		
Computers	X		X		
Chemicals	X	X			
Gas Transmission		X			
Insurance		X	X		
European Off. Prod.			X		
Direct Marketing		X			
Electronics					X
Info. Services	X				X
Insurance	X				X
Chemicals	X		X		
Insurance					X
Financial Services		X		X	X
Medical Supplies	X				X
Specialty Mfg.		X			
Entertainment					X
Software				X	
Total	**8**	**7**	**9**	**4**	**12**

Figure 6.2   *Models Observed in Research Sites*

nization can manage the politics of information from day to day, like an alderman manages a ward. The less mechanistic manager or leader may want to think more about "standing up for information," and changing information sharing and utilization behavior in his or her company.

For a company to succeed in the job of information management, there needs to be a consensus about what information *is* within an organization, who has it, in what form is it kept, who is responsible for its management, and most importantly, how to harness and use the information that exists within all organizations. In fact, the single *key* success factor for real information management is to have a senior executive "stand up for information"—a phrase that was used by a Fortune 500 CEO, in discussion with one of the authors.

But there are few executives who concern themselves with these issues. Since their own information needs are met by their own network and their subordinates, executives' attention to this issue is limited. At one large software company a senior vice-president expressed little interest in the planning for a company-wide information service since, as he stated, "I learn all I need to know from my daily breakfasts with the CEO." The irony of this statement is that, from his perspective, he *does* know all that he needs. His statement also highlights the theme that individuals have valuable information (not just CEOs!). The real question that this story raises is how those who aren't privileged to break bread with the CEO learn the CEO's thoughts. How can information be exchanged within the firm in an unfiltered way—the way that often adds the most value?

A more positive response from a senior executive comes from NYNEX. When AT & T was breaking up, and the "Baby Bells" were being formed, William Eckenrode, a senior executive at the newly minted NYNEX Corporation "stood up for information," insisting that the company have a world-class Information Access Center that would not only contain traditional print resources and database access, but would also be a central repository for such untraditional information resources as the company's experience with consultants (as maintained in written evaluations), and benchmarking results from other units within the company.

Another way in which senior executives can affect an organization's information behavior is to develop positions, or promote executives into positions, of being in charge of information and information processes. This contrasts with the role of a traditional Chief Information Officer (CIO), who usually manages machinery. Xerox, IBM, AT&T, American Express, and McKinsey & Co. are some of the prestigious organizations that have taken this route. This is probably a good thing for some of them, since traditional CIO positions have remarkably short job tenure—the term itself is sometimes even said to mean "Career is Over!"

Technocratic Utopianism

In many companies there is a strong bias to approach information management from a technological perspective. This approach eschews information politics, positing politics as an aberrant form of behavior. It is usually driven by the company's information systems professionals, who see themselves as the custodians, if not the owners, of information. Their technological efforts to alleviate information problems often involve a considerable amount of detailed planning, and revolve around the modeling and efficient use of corporate data. Their goal is to plan a technology infrastructure that can deliver information to each individual's desktop, and then to build databases with the correct structure to store this information without redundancy. Some technical efforts around information management are reasonable; however, when the technological approach to information predominates within a company, its political model of information management can be described as technocratic utopianism.

Technological utopians often have three factors in common: they focus heavily on information modeling and categorization; they place high value on emerging hardware and software technologies; and they attempt to address an organization's entire information inventory.

Technocratic utopians assume that managing information is an exercise without passion. Their rallying cry is an uninspiring, "Data is a corporate asset." They believe, consciously or unconsciously, that the value of information in making business decisions is not only very high, but also self-evident. They assume that employees in possession of information that is valuable to the corporation will share it willingly. But they also assume that information is basically value-less, or at least that its value is the same to all members of an organization. If they are conscious of the relationship between information access and hierarchy, they assume that those high in the hierarchy would not restrict the free flow of information for any reason other than corporate security. These assumptions resemble human behavior found only in utopias.

Anarchy

Some companies have no prevailing political information model, and exist in a state of anarchy. Information anarchy, in which every individual fends for him or herself in terms of information, is only rarely a state that an organization would consciously choose. It usually emerges when more centralized approaches to information management break down, or when no key executive realizes the importance of common information to effective functioning.

Information anarchy was made possible—and much more dangerous—by the introduction and rapid growth of the personal computer. Suddenly individuals and small departments found that they could manage their own databases, and generate their own reports, tailored to suit their own needs at any time they desired, at minimal cost.

The long-term shortcomings of information anarchy are obvious. When everyone has his or her own database, the numbers for revenues, costs, customer order levels, etc., in one database, can quickly diverge from those in another area of the company. Though anarchy is not often chosen consciously, it is not an uncommon syndrome; often it was the source of late or inaccurate quarterly earnings' reports. A company cannot survive for long with such information discrepancies. The desire for information that leads to anarchy should quickly be harnessed into a more organized political model.

Feudalism

The political model most often practiced among the 25 companies studied was feudalism—an environment in which information acquisition, storage, distribution, and analysis are generally controlled by individual executives and their departments.[5] They determine what information will be collected within their realms, how it is interpreted, and in what format it will be reported to the "king," or CEO. These powerful executives can also decide what measures are used to understand performance as well as what common vocabulary is used within the realm. Different realms often end up with different languages, and the subsequent fragmenting of information authority diminishes the power of the entire enterprise—just as the growth of powerful noblemen and their entourages inhibited the power of the king in medieval times.

Feudal actions diminish the power of the central authority to make informed decisions for the common good. Key measures of the health of the enterprise are often not collected, reported, or even considered in any uniform vocabulary beyond roll-up of financial outcomes, which further diminishes the power of the central authority. Corporate-wide performance is of interest only to those within the "corporate division," and may poorly reflect what is actually happening around the company.

Feudalism flourishes, of course, in environments of strong divisional autonomy. When divisions have their own strategies, products, and customers, it is almost inevitable that their information needs will differ from other divisions. Furthermore, they may also be reluctant to fully disclose potentially negative information at the corporate level.

At the U.S. subsidiary of a major consumer electronics company feudalism was quite overt. The company was organized along product lines; heads of each product division were informally referred to as "barons." Each had his own financial reporting system, with only the most limited amounts of data shared with the subsidiary head. The latter executive was eventually led to bring in consultants to give a seminar on the value of common data and systems—unfortunately, to no avail.

At a large consumer goods company organized by distribution channel, each channel had its own way of looking at the business. This information autonomy had prevailed for years, and was tolerated because the company had long been profitable using any set of measures. A new CEO arrived at a time when profits were down and he felt he had no way to manage across the entire company. He mandated the development of a common information architecture. Unfortunately, the IS group charged with this initiative began to create a technological utopia. We suspect that the feudal culture will eventually prevail.

Despite these battles in feudal information environments, some degree of cooperation can emerge. Powerful executives who form strategic alliances to share information or establish a common network or architecture find their analogue in feudal lords who banded together to build a road or common defense wall, or go to war (although, such communally-oriented behavior rarely included all of the lords).

Monarchy

The most practical solution to the problems inherent in the feudal model is to impose an information monarchy. When this occurs in a company, the CEO or someone empowered by the chief executive dictates the rules for how information will be managed. Power over managing information is centralized and the autonomy that departments and divisions have over information policies is substantially reduced.

Much then depends on the approach the "monarch" takes to manage the realm's information. A more benign monarch (or enlightened despot, as they were called in the 18th century) will tilt toward freer access and distribution of key information, and may attempt to rationalize and standardize the parameters used to measure the health and wealth of the state and its subjects.

An example of a benign monarchy occurred at the rapidly growing specialty manufacturer mentioned earlier. The CEO, who felt that information flow was critical to developing a flexible organization, decreed a policy of "common information" in an attempt to open access to consistent information by all who needed it. The appointment of "czars" with responsibility for defining and implementing common information reflected the CEO's belief in the importance of information management issues. The embedding of this decree into a set of business practices and a technical architecture is currently underway. This top-down approach is an example of enlightened monarchy at its best, since the action was not taken in response to a specific crisis but to a broad organizational objective.

A progressive, further step in this direction is a constitutional monarchy. Constitutional monarchy can evolve directly from feudalism or from the more despotic forms of monarchy. As a model for information management, this means that dominion is established over what information is collected, in what form, by whom, and for what ends. The Chart of Accounts becomes the Magna Carta (or Great Chart) of the realm—a document establishing rules that will be enabled by an information technology platform and enforced by processes. A common vocabulary is developed so that the meaning of the realm's information is consistent and has integrity throughout the company. The financial functions at both Digital Equipment and Dow Chemical are establishing constitutional monarchies for financial information, with strong support from the CEO.

One drawback to any information monarchy is the simple fact of mortality. When the monarch dies or is overthrown, a very different viewpoint on information can be imposed on even the most constitutional of monarchies. Cultures and traditions take years to gain a solid hold in an enterprise. In one high-tech manufacturing company the retirement of the founder and CEO led to information anarchy for many years; only now is the company beginning to establish a more structured information environment. The short reigns of most monarchs and CEOs bode poorly for the growth of persistent information traditions.

Federalism

The final information state, federalism, also has a number of desirable features, and in today's business environment it is the preferred model in most circumstances. Its distinguishing feature is the use of negotiation as the lever by which potentially competing and noncooperating parties are brought together. Federalism is the model that most explicitly recognizes the importance of politics, without casting it in pejorative terms. Federalism treats politics, including the politics of information, as a necessary and legitimate activity by which people with different interests work out among themselves a collective definition of purpose, as well as the means for achieving it.

Companies that adopt or evolve into this model typically have strong central leadership and a culture that encourages cooperation and learning. However, it takes tough negotiating and a politically astute information manager to make the federalist model work. He or she needs to have the support of the CEO (though not too much support, or a monarchy emerges) as well as the trust and support of the "lords and barons" who run the divisions. He or she needs to have an understanding of the value of information itself, as well as of the technology that stores, manipulates, and distributes the information. Such skills are not widely distributed throughout organizations, even (or perhaps especially) among information systems executives.

An executive who has this perspective on information can then plan to use cooperative information resources to create a shared information vision. Each duchy can be bargained and contracted to cede some of its information assets in return for helping to create a greater whole—a genuine leveraging of a company's knowledge base.

Larry Ford, the former head of corporate information services at IBM, concluded that IBM needed a dramatically new approach to the way it managed information. Ford and his organization produced an information strategy which focused on the value that information can bring to all of IBM. The strategy was refined and ratified by all senior executives.

Since achieving this consensus, Ford and his staff and the IS executives in IBM's divisions have gone out into the field to negotiate with senior managers about sharing their information with others in the company. "Would you share your product quality data with the service organization? How about sales?" Eventually all the important information will be in easy-to-access "data warehouses." Now, however, information management is a very personal form of politics—like the ward politician, campaigning door-to-door.

Of course, the politician has only so much time to ring doorbells. There may be hundreds of important data elements in one division that need to be shared. IBM is finding that the time it takes to educate and persuade information owners of their responsibilities is the biggest constraint to implementing a federalist model. Ford's departure from IBM to head a software firm may also place the federalist initiative at risk.

Managing Information Politics

Given these options for building an information polity, how do companies begin to effectively manage information? The first step in this process is to select a preferred alternative among the possible information models.

■ *Select an information state*

The first step in managing the politics of information is to know which models are held by people in the firm, which model currently predominates, which model is most desirable, and how to achieve it. Adopting multiple models will needlessly consume scarce resources, and will confuse both managers and users of information. A company should choose a single model and move continually in that direction, however long it takes.

We believe there are only two viable choices among the five models: monarchy or federalism. In a business culture that celebrates empowerment and widespread participation federalism is preferable, but it is harder to achieve and takes more time. Federalism requires managers to negotiate with each other in good faith about information, while avoiding the temptation to use information and the withholding of information in destructive ways.

Figure 6-3 summarizes our assessments of each of the five political models along four dimensions: 1) commonalty of vocabulary and meaning; 2) degree of access to important information; 3) quality of information, (i.e., its currency, relevance, and accuracy); 4) efficiency in the management of information.

Common vocabulary refers to an agreed-upon set of terms, categories, and data elements that carry the same meaning throughout the enterprise. While the desirability of common discourse may appear obvious, it is our experience that this is not the case in many large firms. Even the definition of what constitutes a "sale" can be variously interpreted by different divisions, to say nothing of more ambiguous terms such as "quality," "performance," or "improvement."[6]

The degree of information access is another good indicator of political culture. Many firms proclaim that all employees should have the information they need to do their work well. However, in making the choices about who actually needs what information, they are making political decisions, whether or not they would acknowledge it. The techno-utopians focus less on what information is accessed by whom, and more on the mechanisms of distribution.

In many ways the quality of information is the most important of these indicators. Information quality is achieved

	Federalism	Monarchy	Tech Utopia	Anarchy	Feudalism
Commonality	5	5	3	1	1
Access	5	2	3	4	1
Quality	3	2	1	2	2
Efficiency	3	5	3	1	3
Total	**16**	**14**	**10**	**8**	**8**

Key: 5 = high   3 = moderate   1 = low

Figure 6.3   *Ranking Alternative Models of Information Politics*

through detailed attention to the integrity, accuracy, currency, interpretability, and overall value of the information. Like other types of products, information quality is best judged by its customers. Even companies that declare themselves as firmly in the Information Age, however, rarely have measures or assessments of the quality of their information.

Efficiency in information management is often the objective of technologists who wish to minimize redundant storage of data. The importance of this issue has been reduced somewhat by the improvements in price/performance ratios for data storage technologies. However, there is still a human reason to be concerned about information efficiency. Multiple measures of the same factor take time to analyze and synthesize. Effective management requires focusing on a few key indicators of performance. Computers and disk drives may be able to handle information overload, but people still suffer from it.

Managed properly, federalism has the potential to be effective on all four dimensions of information management. Through negotiations between levels and units, a common vocabulary is established. This makes possible the widespread access and distribution of meaningful information, which is then used for the benefit of the enterprise as a whole. Federalism strikes a balance between the unintegrated independence of the baronies of feudalism, and the fully undifferentiated units under monarchy. Though satisfying all constituencies may lead to the gathering of more information than is absolutely necessary (hence decreasing efficiency), and the necessary compromises may reduce quality, federalism scores higher in the minds of the managers we interviewed than any other model.

Because it explicitly acknowledges the important positive role that the politics of information can play when managed properly, federalism is apt to be the most effective model for companies that rely upon individual initiative for generating collective action. This is most likely to be true for companies operating in complex and rapidly changing competitive environments, which create a high level of uncertainty. The federalist approach to managing information supports both autonomy and coordination. Accomplishing this, of course, requires negotiating skills and the willingness of managers to take the time to engage in these negotiations.

Not all companies have executives with the ability or the commitment to doing this. The temptation always exists to look to a strong monarch to resolve the endless negotiations by fiat, to fall prey once more to the alluring utopian vision painted by the technologists, or to fall back into a nasty and brutish condition of feudal conflict. The difficulties of achieving federalism mean that firms may also want to pursue alternative models, in case federalism fails.

An information monarchy solves some of the problems of managing information throughout the enterprise. A strong top-down approach to information management ensures that there is a common language—in both vocabulary and meaning—underlying the information generated. Little unnecessary information is collected or distributed, guaranteeing a high level of efficiency. The monarch and his or her ministers mandate and oversee that the right processes generate the right information, and that it is used in the right way—all of which enhance information quality, at least as perceived from the top. These advantages, however, are often gained at the expense of information access. It is the rare monarch who has enough democratic ideals to make information as broadly available as it is in a federalist state.

■   *Match information politics to your organizational culture*

It is no accident that democracy emerged in 18th-century America, a sprawling continent with vast resources and an ethic of independence and self-sufficiency. Similarly, the organizational culture within a company must be conducive to participative information management and free information flow before they will happen. Put another way, information flow does not effect a less hierarchical and more open organizational culture; rather, democratic culture makes free information flow possible. When faxes were flying to and from China in the weeks preceding the crackdown at Tienamen Square, some observers argued that the free flow of information was leading to a more open society. Now that the faxes and those who faxed are silent, we know that a democratic culture is a precondition for free information flow, not an outcome.

Information policies are among the last things to change in an organization that is changing its culture. We have never seen increased information flow lead to the elimination of a layer of management, nor have we seen it lead to a greater willingness to share information. When these latter changes happen, they happen for noninformation reasons: restructurings, a strong need for cost control, external events (e.g., the 1970s oil shocks, or the current banking crisis). Several companies, however, state that their new organization could not have survived without new information policies. Phillips Petroleum, for example, radically reduced its management ranks after a raider-forced restructuring. A new information polity was the key to its functioning.[7]

How do you know when your culture is right for more democratic information politics? There are a number of indicators. For example, companies who successfully implement quality programs have to deal with many of the same issues affecting information flow. They have to empower front-line workers to make decisions, work cross-functionally to improve processes, and remove, as much as possible, the use of fear as a motivator. Similarly, companies that are highly attuned to customer satisfaction must be able to deal with negative results in a positive fashion—an essential trait in an information democracy.

Not surprisingly in an era of mergers, acquisitions, and global management, most large organizations can have multiple political cultures with respect to information. A newly acquired company may resist adopting the information-sharing norms of its acquisitor (or as seen in *Barbarians at the Gate*, of its potential acquisitors). Poorly performing divisions will rarely be as enthusiastic about new information reporting initiatives as will long-term strong performers. And geographic differences in the willingness to share information are legendary; how many times has it been uttered, "We're having problems getting data from our French subsidiary."

■   *Practice technological realism*

While technology will not lead to an information utopia, there are still important technological factors to consider in managing information with political astuteness. The engineering of information must be highly focused: information should be in units that managers can understand and negotiate, and technology platforms must be made as common as possible in order for more democratic information models to be successfully achieved.

In negotiating about information, companies may find it useful to use a less granular unit of information than the data element. Most managers do not think in terms of such narrow units: as one executive said with regard to his company's information, "Don't give me all the molecules; tell me the key compounds they can form." A more relevant unit of information may be the document—a form, report, or memo. Technologists must concern themselves with the data elements that appear on documents, but managers will normally be happy not to delve below the level of the document in developing a common information language. Xerox, having designated itself "The Document Company," is beginning to explore how business processes can be supported through documents.[8]

■   *Elect the right information politician*

Along with having a suitable political culture and technology environment, companies desiring to change their information politics must elect (or otherwise get into office) the right information politicians. The role of the information politician—not the *owner* of information, but the *manager* who has primary responsibility for facilitating its effective use—is still up for grabs in many companies, despite some pretenders to the throne. In one fast-growing software company, for example, problems about information flow were widespread, but no one below the CEO took any ownership of the problem.[9] One would assume that the Chief Information Officer would own this domain, but there are a few problems with his or her candidacy.

Until recently most CIOs were selected for technical acumen rather than political skills. Few CIOs have embarked on initiatives to improve the way information—not just information technology—is used and managed in the business. Only a few heads of the information systems function have the political clout to persuade powerful barons to share their information for the good of the entire kingdom. Still, this is changing. At companies such as IBM, Xerox, Kodak, and Merrill Lynch, recent CIOs have been fast-track executives with records of managing important nontechnological aspects of the business. If these nontechnical managers can master the considerable technical challenges in the creation of an information infrastructure, then it appears that they already have the skills and influence to bring about a political environment in which the information can be shared and used.

The Chief Financial Officer is another candidate for information politician. Most CFOs, however, are solely associated with financial information. In order for them to incorporate a broader responsibility for information management, they must at a minimum convince operational executives of their ability to understand and manage operational performance information.

The CEO is perhaps in the best position to lobby for a particular information environment; indeed, in an information monarchy, the CEO is the only politician who counts. In more democratic environments (e.g., federalism) the CEO must appreciate the importance of information and communicate it throughout the firm. The time demands of day-to-day negotiations around information may require that the CEO delegate political authority to other managers.

Like real politicians, the information politician must be both charismatic and organizational. He or she must be able to persuade individuals and the masses of the importance of information management and the correctness of the chosen political model. He or she must also organize a collection of "advance individuals" and "ward heelers" who work every day at building coalitions, influencing opinion leaders, and swaying recalcitrant members of the electorate.

■   *Avoid building information empires*

Because information is such a powerful tool, federalist-oriented organizations will inherently resist or distrust managers who try to amass an empire through broad ownership of information. Concentrating all responsibility for collecting, maintaining, and interpreting information in one executive position is to give too much power to one individual in any organization with democratic leanings. In fact, the concept of information ownership is antithetical to federalist information management. Rather, companies should institute the concept of information "stewardship"—responsibility for ensuring the quality of data, with ownership by the corporation at large. Stewardship of information (again, perhaps at the document level rather than for individual data elements) should be assigned widely throughout the organization.

The IS organization should be particularly careful to avoid building an information empire. It may already wield considerable power by virtue of its technical custody of information. We have observed organizations that cede control over information to this "independent" third party, assuming that it will not use information for political gain. But the IS function may have its own interests to advance, its own kingdom to build.

Conclusion

Using information as a strategic resource, and building processes and structures that will support this focus, is not an activity that lends itself to a mechanistic or schematic approach. It involves having a clear vision of the human aspects and attitudes surrounding information and its usage.

This is not the sort of knowledge that one can easily acquire either from reading about or discussing the issues. It usually comes from accumulated experience working with information in organizations, and is subsequently hard-earned.

Yet, to succeed in understanding and resolving these issues, one needs this sort of experience. Information is not free, nor does it "flow" freely. If it really is a form of wealth, then it is also a form of power, and few can believe that it will be shared within an organization without some serious incentives to do so. It is incumbent on senior management to create an internal management culture that will allow the most beneficial and benign forms of information politics to grow. This is serious work that requires attention at a high level of the organization. Without it, all the careful strategies and practices we have been advocating will come to naught, foundered by the hard rocks of information politics.

Notes

1. This chapter is substantially based on Thomas Davenport, Robert Eccles, and Laurence Prusak, "Information Politics," *Sloan Management Review* (Fall 1992).

2. John Thorbeck, "The Turnaround Value of Values," *Harvard Business Review* (Jan.–Feb. 1991): 52–62.

3. Jeffrey Pfeffer, *Power in Organizations* (New York: HarperBusiness, 1986).

4. A similar term has been defined, without reference to information management, by Howard P. Segal, *Technological Utopianism in American Culture* (Chicago: University of Chicago Press, 1985).

5. Some interesting examples of feudalism, again largely outside of the

information management context, are described in Jeffrey Pfeffer, *Managing With Power* (Boston: Harvard Business School Press, 1991).

6. Some of the reasons for these discrepancies are described in Sharon M. McKinnon and William J. Bruns, Jr., *The Information Mosaic* (Boston: Harvard Business School Press, 1992).

7. Lynda M. Applegate and Charles S. Osborn, "Phillips 66 Company: Executive Information System," 9-189-006 (Boston: Harvard Business School, 1988).

8. See the Proceedings' volume from the Xerox Document Symposium, March 10–11, 1992, Xerox Corporation, Stamford, CT.

9. Julie Gladstone and Nitin Nohria, "Symantec," N9-491-010 (Boston: Harvard Business School, 1990, revised 2/4/91).

PART IV

Linking Design
and Execution:
Measurement,
Feedback, and
Learning

All organizations have strategies. More effective organizations tend to have explicitly designed strategies. Forward-thinking organizations worry about whether these designs are transformed into the resources and operational processes of day-to-day execution.

A fundamental responsibility of management is to create and operate management processes that ensure that strategy design and strategy execution are integrated. How well do day-to-day operations conform to operations called for in the strategy design? Is the organization doing the right things and doing them right? This is the realm of management processes and systems. Management processes include measurement and accounting systems, compensation and reward systems, capital budgeting and resource allocation systems, and internal and external communications systems. Fundamentally, these are all information systems. While holding the greatest promise for improved information management, the use of information technology has had possibly the least impact on management processes and practice. This is perhaps most true in senior levels of management. Viewed from the perspective of providing the integration between design and execution, how should organizations reengineer (or engineer in the first place) their management processes to provide the appropriate feedback throughout the organization? This feedback should be a two-way feedback. Processes need to be designed to better communicate the strategy design throughout the organization and to monitor execution against the design.

In a stable competitive environment, it would be possible for organizations to design their strategy, business processes, and management processes one time. Management processes would only be concerned with monitoring the conformance of execution to the design. In a fully static world that would be the end of the story. In a dynamic world where change is occurring slowly, organizations improve execution processes over time as they accumulate experience. Over long enough periods this execution-level learning may provide feedback that suggests reconsidering strategy designs.

In the rapidly changing environment that constitutes today's competitive world, learning takes on much more central importance. Maintaining effective integration between design and execution may require conscious and explicit adjustments to both the design and the execution of strategy. Instead of relying on adaptive processes and the innate learning capacities of individuals and organizations, learning will have to become an actively managed process.

Valid and timely information is fundamental input to effective learning both by individuals and organizations. This relationship between information and learning forms the final chapter of this section and this book. This is particularly important because improved learning is the most effective route for organizations to take if they wish to implement the thinking we present.

7

Information and Management Processes

Much of this discussion about information and strategy has focused on information's impact on organizations' critical business processes. A second area where information and strategy connect is in an organization's management processes, which include those involved in planning, resource allocation, performance measurement and reporting, compensation, and communication.

Simply by enumerating these processes, the role of information becomes evident. Perhaps too evident. Even the earliest writers of information technology and organization envisioned technology bringing up-to-the-second information from the farthest corners of the enterprise to the executive suite, where its significance could be immediately grasped and appropriate actions taken.

Yet, despite efforts and attention by companies, consultants, and academic researchers, the impact of information technology on the senior levels of organizations has been slight and slow in coming. There are many reasons behind this gap between promise and reality, and there is at least one approach that offers to close it.

Putting technology aside is the first step toward improving the role of information as the link between strategy and execution. The best way of discussing and thinking about this linkage between strategy and execution might be "strategic performance measurement," an umbrella term that encompasses the integration of three components: defining new performance measures, embedding these measures in management processes, and providing a measurement infrastructure (of technology and data scanning, filtering, analysis, and presentation processes).

Before considering the elements of strategic performance measurement in greater detail, it's important to understand why most previous efforts to support executives with information technology have had disappointing results.

The Failure of the Executive Computer

The allure of applying information technology in the executive suite is not hard to understand. It is a quest that began moments after the first application of technology to data processing. Management's role in the organization is to make decisions about today's activities that will yield success in an uncertain future. This has been an information-intensive task from the beginning. "If only we had more data" might be considered the slogan of the contemporary M.B.A.

The success of operations research efforts during and after WW II demonstrated the potential for combining detailed data about organizational processes with rigorous analytical procedures to produce decisions that outperformed experienced and informed management judgment. When computers began to automate basic business processes such as accounting, inventory management, and order entry, it was a simple extrapolation to expect that operations research techniques would be next to sweep through the organization. As with many technical innovations, the pace has been more leisurely, even glacial.

The quest to apply information technology to the executive suite has spawned several streams of important research, countless sales presentations by hardware and software vendors and consultants, and generally disappointing results. In the late 1950s Harold Leavitt and Thomas Whisler described a major role for what they termed information technology in changing the managerial landscape of organizations. Their early definition of information technology encompassed not only the hardware and software technology of the computer but also the intellectual technologies of management science and the promise of artificial intelligence (which probably reflected the generally naive confidence of the time rather than any special insight). They predicted the growth in planning and analysis tasks that are supported by information technology, even though they didn't envision the personal computer or the electronic spreadsheet.

In 1971 Anthony Gorry and Michael Scott Morton coined the term *decision support systems* (DSS). This term allowed organizations to distinguish between the bulk of structured data processing activities, such as recording sales orders or managing payroll, and the use of information and information technology to support the less structured tasks of managers. In turn, decision support systems spawned numerous progeny, including *executive information systems* (EIS), *executive support systems* (ESS), *management support systems* (MSS), *computer-supported cooperative work* (CSCW), and *group decision support systems* (GDSS).

This terminology has been driven both by the marketing strategies of hardware and software vendors who are trying to apply their technology solutions to meet executive information needs, and by academic researchers who are trying to understand applications. Throughout this evolution, under whatever name the technology has appeared, inadequate attention has been paid to information needs.

Certainly, personal computers have found a permanent home in the offices of planners and analysts throughout organizations. Yet, finding organizations that have put this technology to effective use for senior-level general managers is much more difficult. Some academic observers, such as Henry Mintzberg and John Kotter, argue that the tasks and responsibilities of general managers will always limit the direct role of information technology in executive suites; whereas technology innovators continue to argue that success only awaits the next improvements in hardware (e.g., direct-voice input, pen-based computing, large graphical displays, etc.) and decision-support software.

But information *technology* can only become relevant if and when senior executives understand how and why they obtain their information and technology advocates understand how to cater to executives' preferences for obtaining their information from other people.

Strategic Performance Measurement

There is an overriding trend underway that will exert great influence over the use of information technology in management processes: the accelerating effort by organizations to reevaluate their overall approach to the problems of performance measurement and reporting. Buoyed by the successes of the quality movement and business-process innovation efforts, leading organizations in a broad cross section of industries are developing new performance measurements and reporting systems for their executive ranks.

Always a central responsibility of managers, explicit attention to measurement and control waxes and wanes in popular thinking about business performance. Today's business environment has pushed measurement to the forefront once again. As change in the business environment accelerates, organizations are challenged to mesh their competencies and skills more tightly with the environment. In a slowly changing environment there is time for organizations to evolve and adapt their processes to the opportunities presented by the competitive environment. As change accelerates, organizations must actively manage and direct these evolutionary and adaptive processes to ensure an effective fit between organization and environment.

Strategic planning and analysis techniques are the first part of this explicit management requirement. Where it once was possible for an organization to operate from an implicit and unarticulated understanding of its strategic goals and competitive positioning, today strategies must be consciously and explicitly designed and developed. This need has fueled a great deal of academic research on strategy, and has contributed to significant entreprenuerial success by consulting firms offering services to analyze markets and design competitive strategies.

Strategy is both a design problem and an execution problem. Strategic success is not simply a function of insightful analysis and the articulation of new product/market positioning—after reading hundreds of strategic plans, the eyes glaze over the commonalties between them: "first in all markets we serve," "customer focused." What distinguishes leaders from followers is not simply the insights embedded in their strategic plans. Rather, it is their greater capacity for execution, their ability to embed these plans in the organization's day-to-day activities.

The blunt instrument for managing execution is the organization's structure. A common outcome at the end of strategic planning efforts is a reorganization effort. Roles and responsibilities are realigned to reflect new target markets and to support specific initiatives. Unfortunately, reorganization is a slow-moving process. In addition, the disruption in productivity and focus on the organization's members can eliminate many of the potential gains that are hoped for in the strategy analysis.

Many best-selling books about business and management in recent years have addressed this linkage between strategy and execution. This theme has also been considered in much of the academic and research literature. The most promising

Figure 7.1   *Strategic Performance Measurement Linkage*

recent work in this area has been on the concepts of "core competences" and "strategic intent." But what much of this work fails to grasp is the central role of measurement and reporting processes for achieving these strategic goals. People are now beginning to turn to the prospect of using information and performance measurement and reporting as more flexible instruments for improving the linkage between strategy and execution. These strategic performance measurements are the *integrated set of measurements and management processes that link strategy to execution.* Strategic performance measurement is about being more conscious and explicit about creating this linkage between strategy and execution.

Components of Strategic Performance Measurement

Strategic performance measurement encompasses three things:

- An integrated set of performance metrics, encompassing financial and nonfinancial measures.

- Management processes that have been explicitly designed to fit with the metrics.

- A measurement infrastructure to collect, filter, analyze, and disseminate relevant metrics to the appropriate managers within the organization.

Each of these areas has received attention in recent years. However, strategic performance measurement depends on the integration of each of these three areas with the others rather than individual excellence within any one area.

Recently, many have called for new performance measures within organizations, from the "balanced scorecard" to the issuing of a "performance measurement manifesto." What they capture is a renewed interest in performance measures, which addresses the long-known limitations of relying solely on financial measures of performance. But efforts to identify and define new nonfinancial performance measures are inadequate in themselves. Unfortunately, measurement efforts take on a life of their own. Organizations and their consultants get caught up in an effort to define or discover *the* magic measurement.

The successes of the quality movement and the excitement surrounding process improvement and reengineering efforts demonstrate the potential value of well-conceived efforts to improve business performance by systematic efforts to measure and, therefore, understand business processes. The quality movement offers a more balanced understanding of the role of measures in the broader management context. Measurement is the route to developing a deep enough understanding of the business process under scrutiny to suggest meaningful and lasting improvements to the process.

After improvements, measurements allow managers to monitor the process in question on an ongoing basis to ensure that it remains in control. Applying this line of thinking to the processes of managing the organization itself (as distinct from the business process of converting inputs to outputs for sale to customers) leads inevitably to the notion that strategic performance measurement must encompass metrics, management process, and the supporting infrastructure.

Integrated Performance Metrics

The limitations of traditional financial accounting systems in supporting managerially relevant decisions are well known. In thinking about new performance metrics, it is useful to reflect on why businesses came to rely on financial measures of performance. In a simple organization managers can immediately perceive a direct connection between operations and activities and their financial results. With this knowledge they can conceive specific actions and changes to operations that will lead to the financial results they desire. The mental models that link specific operational actions to predictable financial outcomes are simple and robust. They may not even need to be articulated.

But as organizations grow larger and more complex they face a problem. The linkages between operational activities and financial outcomes become longer and more subtle. The models that managers use to guide their actions need to become more complex to reflect the increased complexity of the organization. There are three possible responses to managing this increased complexity.

The first is to collect data and move it through the organization from the point of operation to a manager who can interpret results to take corrective action.

The second is to delegate responsibility for operational decisions to local managers, and assume that local decisions will aggregate to effective overall performance.

These first two choices are the traditional poles of centralization versus decentralization, each with implications for how information about performance will be collected and distributed within the organization. Each of these choices also fails to address some important questions raised by the volatility of the current business environment. This leads to the third possible response that is only now being developed as organizations revisit the issue of performance measures.

This third response revolves around shifting attention from specific performance measurements to explicitly articulating the business performance model the executives believe links operational decisions to financial outcomes. We examine each of these responses in turn.

Response 1: Centralization: Moving Information to the Manager

From an information perspective the first response of centralization can be thought of as a strategy of moving the information to the manager. It assumes that a small core of executives can deal with the issues of complexity as long as the group has access to the requisite information about operational processes.

Prior to the advent of computers and during the early applications of computing technology there was a limit on the amount of data that could be collected and transmitted to the management center. The logical and sensible response was to move summary financial data, since managers understood the relationship between operations and their financial summary.

With greater distance, and more importantly, greater complexity between action and evaluation, the linkage between financial data and operational actions becomes harder to discern. This underlies recent trends toward defining nonfinancial measures of performance. They can be understood as an effort to get back to the actual operational level of understanding that preceded a manager's ability to interpret financial data and craft operational actions that will affect the financial in predicted directions.

Response 2: Decentralization: Moving the Manager to the Information

The second response is to move the managers to the data by decentralizing. This strategy assumes that operational-level decisions require a hands-on understanding of the operational business processes. Connecting operational decisions to financial outcomes is done by holding the decentralized managers to specific financial outcomes. This strategy presents several problems in its own right.

First, many of the actions affecting their financial outcomes are beyond their direct control.

Second, the increased complexity of the environment makes it likely that decentralized managers will find it difficult to link operational actions to financial outcomes, even though these managers are closer to the action.

Response 3: The Technology Compromise: It Doesn't Matter Where the Manager Is

Advances in information technology—both computing and communications technologies—have removed the technical constraints on capturing operational levels of detail data, and have made this detail available to managers. The response by many technologists and suppliers of technical solutions has been to advocate the collection of all possible data about the organization's business events, retaining it in some form of "data warehouse" that managers, whether centralized or decentralized, could then access for performing whatever analysis and diagnosis they desire.

This approach, however, represents an abdication of managerial responsibility. Providing all available operational and financial data is no more helpful than providing only summary financial data.

Why create a problem of information overload to replace the initial problem of information scarcity? Like oxygen, too much or too little information can be fatal. The needs are to manage the information that is made available and the ways in which it is organized.

Matching Measurements and Models

This leads to the third possible response toward defining new performance metrics for the organization. In this response, equal attention is given to identifying the specific measurements to be made and to explicitly articulating the business performance model linking actions and outcomes.

Consider the case of the Texas Eastman Company. Managers of a company chemical processing plant developed simple information systems that restated daily operating decisions in the form of plant and processing department income statements. These statements translated daily operating decisions into financial terms. For example, this system gave operating-level personnel an understandable model of the effects of their decisions to incur overtime to perform a needed repair: it showed that such decisions specifically led to profits in terms of more or higher quality output for the day; and the system generally allowed all the operators and managers in the manufacturing process to share a common model of how operational decisions led to financial results.

By itself, either model—operational or financial—is incomplete. The operational model allows everyone to understand how operating decisions affect operating outputs; how, for example, a repair performed on the second shift allows production to continue on the next morning's shift and produce more output of a given quality. The financial model allows managers to understand what revenues will flow from outputs of a specified quality. Until you put the two models together, however, it's hard for those making the minute-to-minute operating decisions to appreciate their consequences in dollars-and-cents' terms.

Design the Model First

This third response, then, suggests two dimensions to the challenge of defining appropriate performance metrics that will make large-scale organizations manageable in today's environment.

The first dimension requires senior executives in the organization to consciously and explicitly articulate the conceptual model that links the operational actions of the organization to financial outcomes. While it is possible, and useful, to identify the specific characteristics that metrics should display in strategic performance measurement systems (Figure 7-2), it is equally important for the executives of the organization to accept responsibility for articulating and designing a model of the business, within which the measurements make sense. One of the critical responsibilities of senior executives will be to articulate the business performance model. This model will set the rules by which other members of the organization will play.

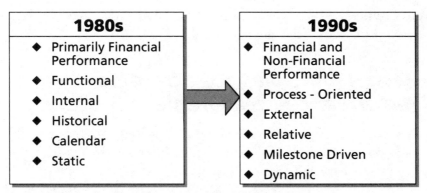

Figure 7.2 *Performance Measurement Characteristics*

Strategic planning and analysis is the first step in this articulation process. It describes and defines the external environment in terms that allow the organization to develop and deploy specific core competences and skills. The process must continue to articulate this model in terms of specific processes, their inputs, outputs, and linkages to other processes.

This definition process highlights points where particular measures can provide early warnings of problems or opportunities. Measurements can then be developed to report on these pertinent process points. This is analogous to the process of designing a temperature gauge for an automobile engine. The gauge provides a relevant performance measurement, including markings to warn the driver of dangerous overheating conditions. But that gauge is useless, and its reports meaningless, unless it is attached to a thermostat, located at a point within the engine where the measurement of temperature has some engineering meaning in the internal combustion design model, which originally governed the development of the engine.

In general, metrics are reflecting the growing complexity of the competitive environment. As long as the environment promises to remain complex, effective metrics must acknowledge and deal with this complexity. The more complex the environment, the more varied and extensive the metrics needed to reflect the environment.

Design Principles for Strategic Performance Measurement Systems

Creating this requisite variety will be a long process for organizations. A number of design principles serve as guidelines for sorting through the complexity:

1. Metrics Must Become Consciously Multidimensional

The increased complexity of the competitive environment dictates that metrics reflect greater diversity. Organizations themselves have always been multidimensional, but in a simpler, slower-paced environment, single measures can meaningfully substitute for the full richness of possible metrics. Demands to create new scorecards reflect this need to elevate multiple aspects of performance for simultaneous consideration. The basic headings for the organization of metrics are constant across a wide range of organizations from Apple to Whirlpool:

- Customer Satisfaction

- Market Share/Performance

- Innovation

- Human Resource Development/Empowerment

- Financial Outcomes

Unfortunately, defining specific metrics for each of these topics depends on the unique circumstances of each organization. As yet, there is no consensus on how to measure these areas, with the exception of financial outcomes. To a large extent, metrics in these areas depend on the particular organization and formation of processes within a unique organization.

2. Organizations Must Explicitly Articulate the Business Model Underlying Their Metrics

All measurement systems represent an implicit theory of how specific metrics relate to outcomes. For example, organizations that measure customer satisfaction do so because they believe that satisfied customers lead to profits. Further, they may believe that product quality leads to customer satisfaction. In most organizations these relationships remain implicit and unarticulated. They are taken for granted. The importance of these models is that they provide a linkage between actions that individuals within the organization can take and outcomes that are desired by relevant stakeholders in the organization.

There are two reasons for making these models explicit in strategic performance measurement systems. First, these models can serve as a communication and management education tool. These models articulate the action levers that executives believe are available to actors throughout the organization. Second, and more importantly, the increased complexity and volatility of the competitive environment increases the risk that the business model will cease to reflect the underlying business reality. The more explicit the model, the easier it will be for executives to use variances in metrics as diagnostic tools to validate and adapt the model to changing circumstances.

3. Organizations Must Place Individual Metrics in Context

In most contemporary U.S. measurement and reporting systems metrics are reported in isolation. Explanations accompanying the numbers are perceived as excuses. By contrast, in a study of Japanese companies' information management practices, numbers were always presented in an appropriate context.[1]

The importance of contextual information is also a function of environmental complexity and volatility. In a stable environment executives will develop a shared context over time as they learn about and adapt to the stable environment. In a complex and volatile environment it may not be possible to develop this shared context rapidly enough without conscious and systematic effort. Therefore it becomes necessary to present metrics within an appropriate and explicit context so that they can be consistently interpreted.

This principle leads to two key characteristics of today's emerging metrics.

First, metrics are increasingly based on data from external sources. For example, organizations such as J. D. Powers and the Gallup organization are using outside suppliers to develop and collect metrics of customer satisfaction.

Second, metrics are increasingly being presented in comparative terms. Market share statistics are the classic example of comparative statistics. Changes in absolute market shares are difficult to interpret until they are recast in terms of changes in relative market share.

4. Organizations Must Treat Metrics as Attention-Focusing Devices Instead of Scorecards

The metaphor of performance metrics as a scorecard can carry unfortunate connotations. Most damaging is that it positions managers on the sidelines, serving as judges. Although certain organizational stakeholders such as shareholders or regulatory agencies may be primarily interested in the "score," managers in today's organizations have a much more important role to play as coaches or mentors.

A track coach doesn't improve a sprinter's performance simply by timing the sprinter through repeated 100-meter dashes. Rather, a coach uses a stopwatch to measure discrete components of the race, such as the start or final kick, in order to find ways to improve each component. Metrics are used in coaching to help focus attention on specific areas in need of improvement.

One implication of this principle is that future performance measurement systems will, of necessity, be more dynamic than today's. The challenge is to clarify this logic to all members of the organization. Managers frequently complain about the "measurement of the month," and feel free to ignore or discount measurement efforts. While this makes sense from a scorekeeping point of view, it is disastrous from a coaching or attention-focusing perspective. As issues evolve, the importance of different metrics will rise and fall within an organization's reporting systems.

Designed Management Processes

Over the last five to ten years there has been increasing emphasis placed on viewing business organizations from a process perspective. Perspectives that emphasize organizational structure are now viewed as contributing to problems of excess specialization and inadequate integration. Much of the success of the quality movement, for example, lies in its emphasis on adopting a dynamic process view of organizational activity. More recently, there has been much talk of the need to radically restructure or reengineer existing organizational processes and procedures because traditional static structural perspectives contribute to a growing gap between environmental change and organizational inertia.

Much of this attention has been focused on core business processes such as:

- Product design and engineering

- Manufacturing and logistics

- Order management and service delivery

This perspective emphasizes rethinking and streamlining business processes to eliminate bottlenecks and duplicated efforts caused by poor communication and poor coordination across the boundaries of conventional business functions.

Despite the exciting results from organizations that have adopted and applied this approach to their business processes, no one appears to have applied a similar perspective to thinking about the managerial processes of the organization. Perhaps this is because management is already considered in process terms, and therefore there has been no motivation to apply new thinking. Perhaps the managers who would most appropriately apply this perspective are reluctant to subject themselves to the same level of scrutiny they have applied to the organization's business processes.

There are, in fact, two reasons for advocating a process view of management.

First, a process view promises performance improvement benefits in management process that are comparable to those achieved in business-process innovation. In many instances business-process innovation efforts have led to significant improvements over current performance.

Second, significant management-process changes must occur if the performance gains from business-process innovation are to be maintained. Business-process innovation achieves its results by breaking down the barriers between existing functions and structures within the organization. If these changes are not accompanied by parallel changes in the core management processes, then these management processes will erode the changes and corresponding benefits instituted during business-process innovation.

Understanding why this is likely depends on identifying the particular organization's management processes. One of the lessons of business-process innovation is that processes are best characterized from a broad perspective, from which high-potential opportunities for change surface. Narrow definitions, such as "closing the general ledger" or "preparing the monthly executive briefing book," perpetuate existing organizational structures and processes. Broad characterizations, such as "business performance assessment" or "stakeholder communication," encourage managers to look beyond the boundaries of current structures. This wider perspective is a necessary precondition for identifying and evaluating substantial redesign of management processes.

The following broad management processes are useful characterizations for considering the evolving role of information in improving management's ability to successfully execute strategy. It is clear from the list that there is substantial overlap between these individual processes when viewed from this broad perspective. Remember that the intent of this perspective is to stimulate thinking about the role of information in making these processes more effectively contribute to the link between strategy and execution.

- **Planning and Budgeting.** This process encompasses current organizational processes of strategic planning, long-range financial planning, annual budgeting, and operational planning. These processes attempt to understand the organization's external environment, identify opportunities to create value, and create a roadmap for guiding and evaluating the organization's progress toward meeting its goals.

- **Resource Allocation.** Within the context of the organization's plans, resources—including capital, technology, people, and management attention—need to be distributed both to the ongoing activities and strategic initiatives of the organization. Viewed conventionally, these processes treat each resource—money, time, people—as discrete. Most of the processes fail to systematically allow for nonfinancial considerations when considering resource-allocation trade-offs.

- **Business Performance Assessment.** Once plans are completed and resources allocated, measuring performance against plan becomes a central management responsibility. Again, in most current organizations, since the plans and resources are developed piecemeal, performance measures are also developed and communicated piecemeal. Thus, separate processes exist to report financial performance, manufacturing performance, human resource performance, project progress, etc.

■ **Stakeholder Communications.** Today's organizations exist in a complex world, with many stakeholders claiming an interest in an organization's performance—e.g., customers, employees, shareholders, the local community, and regulatory authorities. Some of these stakeholders have the power to command certain forms of communication and reporting. Others are important enough to the organization to require specific consideration of their communication needs.

■ **Compensation and Rewards.** The individual managers and contributors in the organization need to be rewarded for performing the specific actions and types of actions that will contribute to the organization's overall success. The recent attention to the perceived equity of executive pay in the U.S. is an example of the challenges to ensuring that rewards encourage the desired behavior in the organization without creating subsequent problems in stakeholder communications.

■ **Process Maintenance and Evolution.** A central management task/process is to guide the ongoing evolution and adaptation of the organization's processes. This process encompasses the balancing act between maintaining the health and utility of the organization's current structures and processes, improving those processes on a continuing basis, and judging where and when to apply business-process innovation thinking and techniques.

Each of these processes needs to be aligned and coordinated with the others and with the organization's business processes. It is the overall level of fit that distinguishes successful organizations—not individual excellence within a particular process. The following principles are design guidelines for creating the management processes appropriate for organizations competing in the next decades:

1. Design Processes Explicitly Versus Accepting the Limits of Historical Evolution

The fundamental impetus behind business-process innovation is the realization that the adaptive and evolutionary way of creating business processes within organizations are inadequate to cope with the increased speed of change in the business environment. The same logic applies to the management processes of the organization. These processes include planning, resource allocation, stakeholder communication, compensation/reward systems, and measurement/reporting.

The solution to this challenge is to design these processes explicitly and consciously. Explicit design provides an opportunity to create processes that maximize value-added activities. It also allows an organization to design processes that can harness its adaptive capacities to keeping processes effectively aligned with the changing environment.

2. Coordinate Management-Process Innovation with Business-Process Innovation Efforts

Business-process innovation efforts refocus the organization on broad business processes that cut across conventional, functional, and even organizational boundaries. They demand new kinds of behavior and cooperation from the individuals executing discrete subprocesses. If these behaviors are to persist, the management processes of the organization must be redesigned to encourage and promote them. If management-process change is not coordinated with business process change, behaviors will revert to what the existing management processes promote and reward.

Although business-process innovation efforts require corresponding management-process innovation to persist, the converse is not true. It is possible for organizations to redesign their management processes without explicitly redesigning business processes, although the value of doing so is unclear.

3. Evolve Metrics from Process Outputs to Process Activities

The general trend in new metrics is to design metrics to promote desired management behaviors in designed business processes. Most existing measurement systems produce metrics of the outputs of discrete business functions. The transition from current state to desired state is too large to be made in a single step. The most promising intermediate step is to develop initial metrics that focus on the outputs of redesigned processes.

Measurement Infrastructure

The third component of strategic performance measurement is infrastructure. Although infrastructure is an overused term, particularly within the information arena, it is a useful umbrella for the supporting procedures, roles, structures, and technologies that calculate measurements and make them available at the right point in management processes.

Within the context of infrastructure the capabilities of information technology become relevant, but only as a part of the puzzle. Improving technology capacities, for example, make it more feasible to collect and store detail data about business events that can be summarized and presented in operational rather than financial detail to managers who are far removed from the events. Whether this is relevant or irrelevant for an organization does not depend on technology capability, but on decisions about how measurements will be used in management processes.

In most organizations, the current measurement infrastructure is an amalgam of multiple infrastructures, which collect and disseminate measurements for a variety of purposes and stakeholders. Some of the measurement and reporting activities that are active at any time within large organizations are: compliance reporting to various regulatory and oversight organizations; financial reporting to the investing public under current accounting and reporting standards; routine management accounting and cost reporting; and ad hoc status and progress reporting against major projects. This amalgam needs to be reexamined in light of the particular measurements and processes called for by a strategic performance measurement perspective.

The following design guidelines promise to lead to measurement infrastructures that effectively capitalize on continuing technology developments and align infrastructure with the information needs of executives, managers, and all employees throughout the organization:

1. Give Priority to Information Needs, Not Availability

Most current reporting and executive information systems are built on the premise that the information contained in existing automated systems is most important. Developers of executive information tools focus on providing more elaborate access to machine-readable data. Measurement efforts that focus on defining new metrics and revised processes are shifting attention to defining information needs irrespective of availability.

2. Focus on Communication and Coordination, Not Computation

The increased attention to process and the use of metrics for coaching and mentoring are making the importance of communication and coordination more evident. Further, the most successful examples of executive information systems have been those that emphasize improving communication and coordination between executives.

3. Seek Robust Approximations, Not Precision

Most reporting systems are based on accounting systems. The double-entry accounting model promotes an artificial precision. The requirements for external reporting perpetuate the need for precision within accounting systems. When organizations make the shift from scorekeeping to diagnostics/coaching measurement systems, the importance of precision diminishes. When metrics are used to support a management dialogue about the action levers that ought to be manipulated, rapid approximations become more meaningful than delayed precision.

4. Create an Executive Information Environment, Not System

Although few organizations express it, examples of effective executive information systems are better viewed as support environments than systems. Thinking of executive information needs in conventional systems' terms places the focus on issues of information technology and software programs. Thinking in terms of the overall support environment shifts attention to less visible, but no less important, elements of the support environment. These include the multiple sources of data and the training and education of the environment's users and support staff, who make the system function on a day-to-day basis. It is the coordination and balance of all these elements that create an effective support environment.

5. Expect Dynamic Evolution

A constant theme throughout organizations' efforts to improve their measurement systems is to maintain effective alignment between the systems and the competitive environment. This means that executive information environments will need to evolve along with the environment. The typical approach to developing executive information environments is to use a prototyping development methodology. The expectation in most organizations is that this development effort ends with the delivery of a working system. A dynamic evolution perspective, however, implies that executive support environments, as opposed to executive information systems, will evolve continually.

Balancing the Components of Strategic Performance Measurement

The balanced emphasis on metrics, process, and infrastructure distinguishes this approach to strategic performance measurement from other efforts. It suggests that the challenges of implementing strategic performance measurement will encompass finding an effective balance among components and implementing new measurement processes in ways that augment an organization's capacity to adapt to changing competitive environments.

The issue of balance, or alignment, is important in several respects. It suggests that quests for the "perfect" measure are unnecessary and possibly counterproductive. Management is a complex, multidimensional, intellectual task (more so perhaps than is usually appreciated by academics and consultants who have the luxury of cheering and criticizing from the sidelines). Measurement and reporting processes should simplify the task, not aggravate it. The goal is not to define a new nonfinancial bottom line. The goal is to introduce metrics that reflect the actual complexity of the competitive environment, without also introducing artificial complexity or confusion. Understanding how product sales differ from one customer segment to another is difficult enough. It should not be made more difficult because one division records weekly sales from Monday to Monday while another records them from Friday to Friday.

"Balance" also means that metrics and measurement processes reflect the information processing capacity of the organization and individual managers. Measures piled on existing measures, or the "measurement of the month," do not improve managers' abilities to cope with information overload. The number of measures and the frequency with which new ones must be introduced need to strike a careful balance between matching the complexities of the environment and exceeding the processing capacity of managers.

A concern for effective implementation is also central to achieving improved strategic performance measurement. Worrying about balance is only part of the implementation problem. Evolving technological capabilities for extracting and reporting data contained in existing information processing systems must be subordinated to the careful assessment of managerial information needs.

Note

1. Laurence Prusak and James Matarazzo, *Information Management and Japanese Success* (Washington: Special Libraries Association, 1992).

8

Information and the Learning Organization

Learning has become a central task for organizations that hope to compete effectively in today's business environment. It's possible that the concept of organizational learning has already achieved the status of conventional wisdom, eliminating any responsibility for managers to think about its implications. But that would be unfortunate. There is a long academic tradition about the importance of the learning organization. Every observer of organizations we can think of has stressed the importance of learning in one way or another. This chapter examines the particular roles that information, information technology, and the information management process play in improving an organization's ability to learn.

Why Organizational Learning is Increasingly Important

All organizations learn. What is at issue is the increasing need to be more explicit, systematic, and efficient at learning. Webster's defines learning as the "modification of a behavioral tendency by experience." At this simple level learning is the process through which an organization adapts to its environment, much as living organisms adapt to their environments. Organisms, and organizations, that do not adapt to their environment—that do not learn—do not survive.

In stable, slowly changing environments, learning and adaptation can proceed slowly. Trial and error is an effective, and possibly the most appropriate, learning strategy. In unstable, rapidly changing environments, explicit, systematic learning must be the linchpin of strategies to keep organizations adapted to their environment (See Figure 8-1).

Learning is both the impetus and engine for change. As the impetus for change, learning is about watching the environment for soft or weak signals that present early warnings of threats or opportunities. It is about detecting changes that

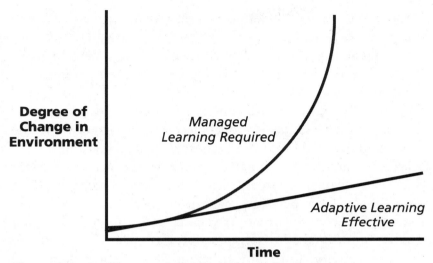

Figure 8.1 *Environmental Change and Learning Strategies*

threaten to widen the gap between the environmental demands and the organization as it currently operates.

As an engine for change, learning provides processes to
close the widening gap. Learning is central to analyzing and
describing the gap between environment and current practice,
identifying models and exemplars of other organizations' responses to similar gaps, designing changes to current organizational practice to bridge the gap, and providing processes
and tools to propagate change through the organization.

Senior management has a central role and responsibility
in supporting and valuing learning that occurs in the organization. This occurs primarily through the explicit recognition
and acknowledgment by senior management that learning is
vital for the organization's life. In *The Fifth Discipline*, Peter
Senge writes that "learning disabilities are tragic in children,
but they are fatal in organizations." Executives must encourage
and reward efforts, experiments, and resource allocations that
enable and encourage organizational learning. It's not enough
to promote learning in the annual report or mention it in a
speech. Learning must be explicitly sought out and valued

throughout the organization. Openness to new ideas, and openness to learning is vital. Without top-down support, individual and organizational learning is too haphazard to effectively close the gap between today's environment and the organization.

Providing an environment that values and encourages learning by individuals is the single most important thing the organization can do to leverage organizational learning. In research on Japanese information management, it became clear that many Japanese executives spent time reading at their desks, really learning. How many Americans feel comfortable reading at their desk; reading a book, not a memo or even a report, but a book? Very few people say, "This is a valuable business activity, I'm going to spend three hours of my day reading this article, reading this book because it's relevant and it's reflective and it will teach me something."[1]

Forms of Systematic Learning in Organizations

It is not our purpose to exhaustively review what has already been written on organizational learning. But various forms of learning in the organizational context need to be briefly described in order to understand the particular role of information, information technology, and information management. It's useful to separate the learning that occurs by individuals in organizations from the ability of organizations to capitalize on and leverage individual learning.

Individual Learning in Organizations

At the individual level learning is something that occurs simply by virtue of being human. We do it all the time. What's changing is the need to harness and exploit that capability more systematically and explicitly to meet the demands of today's jobs.

Within this context learning is about acquiring new skills and perspectives, not about acquiring new facts. To benefit the organization, individual learning must translate into the ability to do or think new things that can be translated into relevant actions for the organization.

Take the simple example of individual reading habits, from a learning perspective. To generate useful (i.e., actionable) organizational learning, individuals ought to pursue greater variety in their selection of material to read; to seek what ecologists and biologists call *requisite variety*. Coping with the richness and complexity of the competitive environment requires a matching richness and complexity in the organization's knowledge and perspective. One tool for developing this requisite richness in perspective is to seek out multiple inputs and perspectives by reading widely.

As people get older, they tend to read things that confirm the way they look at the world. They don't seek out new ways of looking at the world. The business publications that most executives read most of the time confirm how they view the world. Although this kind of reading can present relevant data, its learning value is low. There is greater value in reading outside the standard business mainstream, which can be as simple as occasionally reading trade magazines in industries that are foreign to you, or as complex as starting to study a topic far afield, such as biology or history.

Essentially, this is an argument for the practical value of a continuing liberal education. The practical value lies not in the specific knowledge but in the alternative ways of looking at the world. These alternatives can suggest creative solutions to problems that have resisted conventional wisdom within an industry or organization.

"Thinking outside the box" is a phrase that frequently crops up when organizations try to invent innovative solutions to vexing problems. That means having something to think about. Almost twenty years ago, the current CEO of Citicorp, John Reed, achieved notoriety and significantly improved Citicorp's back-office operations by thinking about them as a "factory" for processing paper.

Most of the recent talk about paradigm shifts is an effort to encourage individuals in organizations to go back to the kind of learning that occurred when they were in school. Eric Hoffer captured the essence of this argument in very simple terms:

> In times of change, learners inherit the earth, while the learned find themselves beautifully equipped to deal with a world that no longer exists.

Learning at the Organizational Level

While there is much learning at the individual level that enhances organizational richness, there are other forms of learning at the organizational level.

Organizations learn in two ways. First, organizations learn from the ways they support or promote learning by their individual members. Most of the learning capacity of the organization is tied up in the learning capacity of its individual members, whose learning increases their ability to contribute to the organization's goals. Second, organizations learn from the ways they create systems and relationships to leverage individual learning to meet broader organizational goals.

There is obvious organizational support of individual learning in the form of training and educational seminars and sessions. In some industries and professions such as medicine, engineering, and public accounting, continuing education is a formal requirement for continued certification. Training and education budgets are rising in many industries, with some organizations going as far as setting up their own internal educational systems, complete with campuses, faculty, and curriculum. Much of this investment focuses on making the distribution of current organizational knowledge, such as sales techniques or consulting practices, more efficient.

What organizations do in terms of offering informal support for daily learning, or creating a generally supportive atmosphere for learning is equally, if not more, important than formal training processes. For example, one Japanese pharmaceutical company provides a "talking space." This is a large, comfortable room that is reserved for research staff to gather for "intellectual exchange"; a place in which they can discuss a new concept or something they just read, or simply jump-start their thinking. Offices and conference rooms equipped with whiteboards are another simple example of informally promoting and encouraging learning.

Organizations themselves are also capable of learning ways to carry out new tasks and functions. Organizations learn how to deliver services. Organizations learn how to manufacture products. That's learning created from the collective learning of individuals. There's no single individual at General Motors who knows everything that needs to be known to manufacture a Saturn. That knowledge and learning is embedded in the organization's systems, structures, and processes.

Managing Information and Information Technology to Enhance Organizational Learning

What role do information and information technology play in leveraging, supporting, and enabling learning in organizations? Peter Drucker suggested one role when he defined information as "data endowed with relevance and purpose."[2]

The formal information systems in most U.S. organizations primarily focus on collecting and disseminating valid data, i.e., accurate facts about the organization and its environment. But data by itself isn't enough. Data doesn't become information until the relationships between the various facts and their implications for the organization and the individual are brought out, made visible, and made explicit. When you have both valid data and an understanding of the relationships within the data, then you can be said to have something resembling information.

Making Contextual Information Explicit for Learning

The failure of information systems in organizations is that, at best, they present valid data; however, in many systems there are questions as to whether the data is valid. The relationships, context, and implications of the data for the organization— what turns the data into information—are developed either in the individual manager's mind or in a presentation or report prepared by a lower-level analyst.

Contextualizing data is where learning occurs. The Japanese term for information emphasizes this intimate linkage between information and learning. It is a much more active term, implying knowledge and action. To a Japanese businessperson it's considered contrary to present raw data without placing it in a context. This cultural emphasis on relationships flows into business. A Japanese analyst would never simply present: "This company had a net loss for this quarter." Instead, the presentation would be more subtle: "Let's discuss this company's performance in terms of how it's been doing historically, the variables, and the environment."

This approach emphasizes individual and organizational learning by calling greater attention to context. Raw facts in isolation are meaningless. You have to see the relationships. When information systems provide only raw data, system users supply the necessary relationships as implicit mental models.

This impedes learning, both for individuals and the organization.

Return for a moment to the business review meeting, in which the first half of the meeting was spent arguing over the number for last month's sales—not what to do about the sales number; not what the sales number means for us—but simple disagreement as to what the "fact" is about sales. In a system that only provides raw data, without proper context, everyone applies a different model for what constitutes sales. The sales manager's version is, "What have we booked for the month?" The production manager's view of sales is, "What has gone into inventory?" or "What has gone out of inventory?" And the accounts receivable manager's view is, "What money have I collected?"

Each of these answers is based on a different model of performance. These models provide the linkages between the simple "fact" and its implications for action. These models, not the data, determine how individuals will respond. The organization's response flows from netting out the individual actions of multiple managers. Some actions will reinforce one another, some will cancel each other.

The problem of reaching consensus on the facts is the focus of information architecture. The first problem to solve is to get everyone to begin from a common starting point. The preceding chapter focused on the second problem: creating effective models that show how measurements and data are linked to action. **The learning problem is to make this contextualizing process visible and explicit, so that the contradictions and inconsistencies in different performance models can be examined and reconciled.**

Learning is enhanced by making contextual issues at least as obvious, explicit, and visible as the facts, because the facts can't be interpreted without the context. Shared context, or shared performance models, imply that the actions taken around the organization in response to a given fact will be consistent. Context is how the right hand knows what the left hand is doing.

In most organizations the problem of creating shared context is solved by the slow process of communicating organizational culture to managers and employees. This is one of those slow, adaptive processes that has become less viable in today's more volatile environment. Actively articulating and communicating contextual information within information systems can amplify this adaptive process and make it a learning process that can be managed.

Understanding, from a learning perspective, how information must be considered as both valid data and the contextualizing relationships among them leads to inevitable questions: "How can one leverage information and information technologies to improve the learning that goes on in an organization?" "How can an organization use information and information technology to improve the learning of individuals within the organization?" "How can an organization use information and information technology to leverage learning for the organization—to capture individuals' learning to the ultimate benefit of the organization?"

Leveraging Individual Learning

There are several ways in which organizations can improve the learning ability of individuals. One way is to improve access to valid data. A second way is to provide tools, for thought and reflection, for communicating what individuals learn, and for testing and experimenting with learning at low organizational cost. A third way is to improve access to other learners and teachers within and outside the organization. This third aspect will be taken up in the next section.

Improving access to valid data has been the underlying argument for substantial investments in information technology within organizations and for the marketing success of vendors of decision support tools and executive information and support tools and software. Little learning of value to the organization can occur until there is some agreement about the underlying facts.

A by-product of efforts to create new transaction-processing systems in many organizations has been to improve the basic quality of the data captured and recorded. Equipping drivers at Frito-Lay with handheld computers has certainly improved the productivity of individual drivers and, by some accounts, has led to improved competitive positioning for Frito-Lay. A less emphasized benefit has been that marketing executives and general managers throughout the organization now have much better access to valid data about business events. The learning process advances when discussions can move from debates over the facts to debates over interpretations about the facts. Learning also improves when the fear that information politics has distorted the shared facts diminishes, because everyone can refer to a common source for the facts.

Although simply improving access to data helps individual learning, the more important application of technology has been the emergence of tools to leverage the learning capabilities of individuals. Much of the personal computing technology introduced over the last decade can be thought of as tools to improve the learning capacity of individuals within an organization. Too often these tools have been perceived only as ways to improve the productivity of individuals, improving their ability to turn out more budgets or more memos. Properly used, however, these tools permit managers to explore more alternatives about a budget and learn more about the models embodied in the budget.

The facts are only part of the puzzle. Information and information technology also provide better access to models that improve the learning process. Models have, at best, a mixed reputation in most organizations. Formalized operations research and management science models have proven to be powerful tools for solving complex problems. These tools use computer technology to manage the volumes and complexity of data that overwhelm human decision makers. At the same time, the human capacity for recognizing patterns in complexity still surpasses the capabilities of formal tools and techniques to handle poorly structured or emergent problems.

Many executives are threatened by the power of models to address complex problems. Executives who are not threatened still question the relevance of formal models on the basis of their limitations in the face of unstructured complexity. These conceptual models, however, serve a second, learning, purpose that transcends their power to solve specific business problems. As models, they impose a structure on the complexity of raw business events, which permits humans to learn new skills for interpreting and acting on the environment.

Learning Through Models

This learning value of models is exploited in formal business school courses on operations research and management science. However, this value becomes lost in organizations because of the complexity of applying the tools to real problems and the costs of implementing these models on large-scale computers. An under-exploited opportunity in today's advancing personal computer technology is to recapture the learning value of complex modeling and simulation of real-world events using computer-based systems.

Simulation and modeling techniques demonstrated their power with the success of operations research methods during and after WW II. The techniques also briefly flourished with the earliest developments of computer technologies, which eased the computational demands of these techniques. Although basic management science and operations research techniques are taught in most M.B.A. programs, their use has been largely relegated to specialists within a handful of organizations. This is partly a function of an unfortunate focus on the results of these models instead of a focus on their value as tools for learning and experimentation. Perhaps managers quietly fear losing their status if mathematical tools promise optimum answers to problems. If the competitive environment continues to evolve at its current dynamic rate, there is little likelihood that answers from simulation models will threaten human decision makers.

A spreadsheet program is a very simple example of the power of personal computer technology as a simulation and learning tool. Although its usefulness as a planning and budgeting tool has overshadowed its value as a learning tool, there are still important lessons to draw about learning from spreadsheets that are enabled by personal computer technology.

First, spreadsheets did not add significant function to tools that were already available on larger scale computers. It was possible to develop and maintain financial plans and budgets using tools such as IFPS (Interactive Financial Planning System) on mainframe and minicomputer technology. However, these larger scale tools had limited impact on the broader organization, largely because their underlying technology made them poor learning tools, regardless of their strengths in functional terms. Even the limited capabilities of the first computer spreadsheets, such as Visicalc, were more valuable to both individuals and organizations because they made the computerized budget models visible and manipulable. Both the individuals developing the models and their colleagues in the broader organization were able to interact with the developing model. This interaction supported shared learning about the assumptions underlying the model, which led to the possibility of developing models that better mirrored the external environment and broader organization. Although spreadsheets *did* less than other available tools, the spreadsheets presented the tools' capabilities in a way that was much more conducive to learning than more functionally capable tools.

The ability to pose and answer "what if" questions has always been a marketing feature of modeling tools. For two reasons, the promise was best realized in spreadsheet tools running on personal computers. First, "what if" questions lead to most effective learning when the answer arrives while the question is still fresh in a manager's mind. The highly interactive nature of personal computers amplified their learning value. And their value was further amplified over the learning value of time-sharing modeling tools because of the economics of personal computers. There were no incremental costs to extended interactions. Once the PC and spreadsheet were paid for, all future modeling sessions were effectively free.

This is important because it is the interaction process that leads to greater insight and learning from the tools. In other words, the learning value of these tools lies in the model development and refinement process, not in the specific output results. Because the learning occurs during model development and refining, it is important that the user be able to try out hypotheses and unusual model structures with the comfort that false starts and dead-end paths won't be sources of embarrassment. The relative privacy of desktop models encourages a more experimental attitude, which will contribute to greater learning.

The second advantage of spreadsheet tools was the simplicity and visibility they brought to the models themselves. With a spreadsheet tool, it is as easy to modify the structure of the model as it is to alter the value of individual data parameters. In the early stages of learning with models, both the data and the model need to be easy to modify.

Other simulation and planning tools that tap the interactive power of personal computer technologies in ways similar to spreadsheets are beginning to emerge. The simulation of dynamic processes, such as factory assembly lines, has been possible with large-scale computing technology for some time. This capability has only limitedly been used within many organizations, the usual reasons being the cost and complexity of building such models. But, much of the reluctance to use these tools is really a function of their inaccessibility. The success and popularity of PC simulation games, such as SimCity and SimEarth, offer a hint of the likely value of simulation tools as they become more widely available in interactive, engaging implementations.

As a culture, we value experiential learning. Touch and do is much more lasting learning than listen and read. Although experiential learning is a very valuable kind of learning, our culture overemphasizes experiential learning at the expense of theoretical or conceptual learning. One of the things that information technology can do, particularly in the interactive forms illustrated by spreadsheet models, is to capitalize on our love for experiential learning by simulating more theoretical kinds of knowledge. Translating abstract theories into interactive simulations makes theories tangible, discrete, and more real to the typical manager.

Computer simulations and management games allow individuals to try low-cost experiments without risking harm to the organization. "What if I applied this theory about how my advertising budget relates to sales?" Rather than spend half a million dollars in a market test to understand the potential applicability of some new theory, information technology lets you simulate that theory as a low-cost way to persuade the organization that the theory is applicable before committing great sums of money.

Sharing and Disseminating Individual Learning

While information technology can enhance individual learning within the organization in many ways, a more important task is to capture that knowledge to the benefit of the organization. That occurs in several ways. One way is by improving coordination, communication, and collaboration among individuals so that the expert knowledge and learning of individuals within the organization can be transferred from the individuals with knowledge to individuals who need or can take advantage of that knowledge. A second way is by developing methods to capture and preserve individual experts' learning outside of the memories and experiences of those experts. While many organizations acknowledge that their most important assets walk out the door at night, few have systematically sought other ways to capture and preserve that expertise.

Improving communication and coordination of information are processes that are critical to extending individual learning to the broader organization. Again, an example from Japanese practice is pertinent. In one particular company individual sales representatives are required to write trip reports as they call on accounts. In itself, this is not terribly different from common American practice; yet, the emphasis is on understanding why customers placed their orders and what they were thinking, as gleaned from the information gathered during a sales call.

In an atmosphere that values learning, such trip reports can be a valuable tool for individual sales representatives. It allows them to reflect on their sales efforts and improve them over time. But this company went a step further in making this contextual information more broadly available to the organization. Not only did the company require sales representatives to prepare trip reports, but the finished reports were disseminated throughout the organization as a source for important and valuable knowledge about particular customers. In this particular organization it was important for everyone to understand more about what customers were thinking than what they had ordered in order to answer questions such as: "How does this information about what my customers were thinking of doing with my products influence what goes on in engineering/design, what goes on in manufacturing, what ought to be going on in marketing, or perhaps what should go on in accounting?"

In this same organization when sales representatives or engineers go to a conference, they come back and hold a three- or four-hour meeting with everyone else who is interested in the subject to discuss what they learned—not only learned in a theoretical sense—but who else was there, what they were saying, which companies were represented. In the U.S., this rarely happens. People go to conferences but their organizations do little to extract greater value from the learning that occurs there. More often than not individuals return from a conference, throw the conference report on a bookcase, and throw business cards into a drawer. Rarely do people write about what they learned and circulate it so that it becomes part of the organizational knowledge base. That is not leveraging learning.

Another way organizations can institutionalize learning is through internal education. And this means creating real learning opportunities, not simply training people. Most consulting firms, for example, regularly set aside time for their employees to convene and wrestle with substantive issues of importance to their practices. Several large organizations have created their own internal colleges and universities with campuses and full-scale curricula.

Although valuable, these efforts are predicated on an assumption of relative stability, which is less and less apparent in today's competitive environment. These institutionalized learning efforts are designed to leverage the transfer of stable learnings by a few experts to the broad reaches of the organization. Lessons from successful projects are codified into standard approaches and methodologies for application to all future projects. These strategies are less valuable when a high percentage of the organization's work force needs to be actively involved in generating new learning, rather than simply drawing from the learning of a few individuals.

Xerox has recently begun to describe itself as the "Document Company." As part of the transition process, Xerox held a week-long symposium on what documents mean to organizations, how they play a role in processes, and how they play a role in the life of a business. The company assembled both external and internal expertise, gave out a great number of books and articles, and invested substantial time and resources in creating a forum for key managers throughout the organization to think through the large issues surrounding this change. All of the participants were actively engaged in the learning process.

Electronic mail, computer conferences, and the recent market success of products such as Lotus Notes are further examples of what can be done at an organizational level to improve information sharing for learning, while also preserving a record of the learning that can benefit the organization as a whole, not just the individuals who participated in the initial learning process. There is frequently as much or more value in understanding the line of reasoning behind a decision as there is in the decision itself. The various information technologies lumped under the broad heading of "groupware" or "computer-supported cooperative work" have learning value by preserving a record of the learning process, which can be reviewed after the fact. New members of the organization can understand and appreciate old decisions by going back to the records. And this shortens the process that now occurs principally at the knees of the masters.

Translating Learning Processes into Business Value

A handful of organizations are moving beyond thinking about learning processes as something of broad general value to the organization toward creating learning processes that lead directly to economic value for the organization. Many of these examples are initially appearing in customer service and sales organizations.

For example, Dell Computers has grown rapidly by marketing personal computers on a mail-order basis. From their earliest days the company has used information technology to directly support learning processes that both leverage the strengths of a mail-order strategy and compensate for its weaknesses. When a prospective customer contacts Dell about a possible purchase, the information from this initial call is captured and stored in a computer database. Since a sale may entail several phone calls over a number of weeks, this information-enabled sales strategy allows any one of Dell's customer-service representatives to have the complete history of the prospective customer whenever a call is made. This allows Dell to provide individualized service to the customer and to gain a high level of productivity from its customer-service representatives. These systems also make it easier to bring new sales and customer-service representatives up to speed.

In a number of software companies, similar technology is being used to leverage learning across technical-support personnel. Both Microsoft and Wordperfect, for example, maintain textual databases of reported software problems and solutions. These databases are available to technical-support staff who take calls from users. By recording this information centrally, these databases leverage the learning of each technical-support person manyfold. As solutions to particular problems are found, they become widely available to the entire technical-support organization.

This strategy is not limited to high technology organizations. Otis Elevator uses a similar approach with its Otisline system, which dispatches service technicians nationwide from a centralized telephone dispatching service. In addition to using a database that is organized by elevator site to record trouble reports and repairs for the benefit of dispatching service technicians, Otis further extracts learning value from this system by analyzing the repair history of particular elevator models and installations in order to schedule preventive maintenance and to compile feedback to the design engineering function for the development of more reliable and serviceable elevators.

All of these organizations succeed by creating explicit processes to capture information and expertise. Positions are created to understand information that is relevant to the organization, and then to capture it, analyze it, and disseminate it. By institutionalizing these processes, organizations are able to capture the learning of individual customer-service representatives or service technicians and make that learning more broadly available to others in the organization who can also derive benefit from this learning.

Measuring Progress at Creating Learning Organizations

How can an organization know whether learning is actually occurring? It's one thing to provide everyone with a subscription to *Business Week*, or give everyone in the organization a seminar budget, or even ask them to read a book. It's another to understand whether or not any learning has occurred within the individual and whether any of that learning has been captured to organizational advantage.

The successes of the quality movement suggest one approach to measuring and evaluating learning and the effectiveness of learning processes. Data about learning can be collected in surveys or interviews. The goal is to obtain continuous and in-depth feedback from the people whose learning mattered in order to use it as input for the development of particular learning processes.

An example is the information management process at British Telecom. At British Telecom's large research laboratory in Ipswich, England, the head of the research library was trying to get more users and have more effect on the organization. He used his own budget to sponsor a buffet lunch, once a week for a month, as an alternative to the cafeteria lunch. He posted a sign that read, "A better lunch is available here." People came and he asked them to fill out questionnaires to the effect, "What are we doing right; what are we doing wrong?" This method provided a source of data, or learning, about how to improve a particular learning process within an organization.

Regardless of good intentions, there is a danger to evaluating individual learning in organizations: trying to micromanage the process. Trying to assess the particular contributions of specific learning activities runs counter to the intent of promoting a broad organizational orientation to learning. Trying to determine whether a particular book or magazine subscription contributes to learning is difficult, if not impossible. Polling individuals within the organization about their perceptions of learning value may be the most straightforward and robust approach.

Simply ask people, either in periodic interviews or surveys, "How valuable was this to you? Did it help you understand your environment better? Did it help you understand your organization better? Do you feel more informed? Has your potential been enhanced? Do you have a better grasp of the relationship of your organization and the interface with all the environmental factors?" Periodically asking these types of questions serves two functions. First, it provides feedback that can help those charged with promoting learning to adjust and improve their processes. Second, the act of asking these questions is demonstrable evidence that learning is a valued activity.

Learning, Productivity, and Strategy

This chapter could just as easily have been the first chapter as the last. In a stable, slow-changing world organizations can stick with a strategy and let evolution take its course. Changes in design, execution, or integration can be made cautiously, with the security that there will be time to adapt.

But in the contemporary economic environment, organizations that cannot adapt rapidly and consciously die. Producing an effective solution to the strategy problem of design, execution, and integration depends on the effective use and management of information. Producing subsequent solutions as the environment changes depends on learning. And learning depends on the effective use and management of information.

Although ubiquitous, information cannot be taken for granted. Nor can responsibility for it be delegated. Each and every member of the organization must take active and explicit responsibility for the effective use and management of information.

Notes

1. Laurence Prusak and James Matarazzo, *Information Management and Japanese Success* (Washington: Special Libraries Association, 1992).

2. Peter Drucker, "The Coming of the New Organization," *Harvard Business Review* (Jan.–Feb. 1988).

Bibliographic Essay

"Of the making of books, there is no end," and certainly there will be no shortage of books on the subjects of strategy and information in the decades to come. However, we would like to freely acknowledge our dependence and debt to the many researchers, writers, and teachers who have attempted to think through differing aspects of these subjects and who have subsequently influenced our own thinking and research for this volume.

It has always been a disappointment to us, when reading an interesting book, to find a bibliography that only lists citations, rather than a sentence or two explaining why a particular book is being cited. For example, entries under the heading, "Further Reading," at the very least should provide the rationale for including a particular volume. This proves especially true when the reader, due to time or interest constraints, must quickly locate certain offerings from the subject's vast literature. It is at this specific point (the point at which we assume many of our readers to be) that annotations can prove most valuable.

One final note: this essay only deals with books and reports, not individual articles, because many key articles in these fields have been expanded into books or collected in anthologies. Those articles that have played a substantial role in our thinking but that do not appear in this essay are listed in the footnotes.

Journals

No journal that we know specifically focuses on the relations between strategy and information. However, several publications consistently include articles with considerable relevance to these subjects. This is certainly true of the well-known *Harvard Business Review, Sloan Management Review,* and the *California Management Review.* The *International Review of Information Management* and the *MIS Quarterly* often have articles of interest on managing and using information strategically. The *Academy of Management Review* is academic and often dry, but it, too, periodically produces some interesting pieces, often with a sociological perspective. *Long Term Planning* is good for "pure" strategy pieces, while *Planning Review* focuses on the more operational aspects of strategy execution.

Several journals seek to focus on "strategic systems," however these are defined. The better ones are: *Journal of Information Systems*; *Journal of Management Information Systems*; *Journal of Strategic Information Systems*; and the *European Journal of Information Systems.* However, in differing levels, they all tilt toward presenting a purely "systems" approach.

Another field that attracts researchers to strategy and information is organizational behavior. For our purposes the key journals are *Organization Science,* and the *Journal of Organizational Computing.*

Scientific American does a good job of covering emerging technologies and technological issues from a nonpartisan point of view; so does M.I.T.'s *Technology Review*. In addition, the science section of the *New York Times* frequently covers information technology applications.

There are a number of more general periodicals that offer insights into the issues discussed here, though perhaps with less frequency and less intent. *The Economist* covers information and strategy topics with a characteristic skepticism and style. This consistently interesting magazine produces supplements, management briefings, and cases covering company decisions, which are almost always worth reading. From time to time, *Fortune* magazine publishes articles about business issues and corporations, which can be valuable. Their articles tend to be more valuable the more analytic they are. *CFO* and *CIO* magazines attempt to cover some of these topics from a senior executive standpoint. For alternative viewpoints, often useful for "early warning" alerts, try *Whole Earth Review* and the *Utne Reader*.

Setting the Stage

The works of Alfred Chandler offer the widest historical and global examinations of how American business got where it is today. His three classic volumes are: *Strategy and Structure: Chapters in the History of the American Industrial Enterprise* (Cambridge: The MIT Press, 1967), *The Visible Hand: The Managerial Revolution in American Business* (Cambridge: Harvard University Press, 1977), and *Scale and Scope: The Dynamics of Industrial Capitalism* (Cambridge: Harvard University Press, 1990).

Peter Drucker's books are more discursive, though no less valuable than Chandler's. He has been writing since the early 1950s and his books provide a running and insightful commentary on business strategy and operations. Lately, his works have had an information orientation, which makes them especially relevant to our own aims. Try: *Management: Tasks, Responsibilities, Practices* (Oxford: Butterworth–Heinemann Ltd., 1974), *The Age of Discontinuity: Guidelines to Our Changing Society* (New Brunswick: Transaction Publishers, 1992), and *The New Realities* (New York: Harper & Row, 1989). Charles Handy, who is the U.K.'s analogue to Peter Drucker, sums up his thinking on the current business situation in *The Age of Unreason* (Boston: Harvard Business School Press, 1989).

Two very recent books published by our colleagues provide unique perspectives on strategic and informational issues that have had a significant influence on our own thinking, as reflected in this book. In *Beyond the Hype* (Boston: Harvard Business School Press, 1992), Professors Robert Eccles and Nitan Nohria show, among other things, how language in business specifically shapes subsequent actions, and that even strategy can be seen as a "language game." Tom Davenport's *Process Innovation: Reengineering Work through Information Technology* (Boston: Harvard Business School Press, 1992) is the first serious attempt to systematically analyze one of the "hottest" topics sweeping through business. Davenport analyzes the relations between process, information, information technology, and the opportunities presented by adopting this perspective.

Strategy Formulation and Design

The concept of strategy has its origins in military thinking, and until fairly recently, it was used more in the sense of a particular general's aims than for describing the actions of an organization. Judging by the business best-seller lists this perspective has not been forgotten, as long-neglected tomes by Chinese generals and Renaissance couriers become guides to current actions. Militaristic strategy perpetuates the belief that the best metaphor for an organization is one of warfare—a focus that we do not promote in this text. However, to understand this perspective from an analytical and learned point of view, read B. H. Liddell Hart's *Strategy* (New York: Praeger, 1969).

A good contemporary starting point for understanding current business strategic thinking is J. I. Moore's *Writers on Strategy and Strategic Management* (New York: Penguin Books, 1992). It presents a useful collection of essays on most of the major strategic thinkers within academia and consulting. Derek Abell's *Defining the Business: The Starting Point of Strategic Planning* (Englewood Cliffs: Prentice Hall, 1980) offers a design perspective on competitive strategy which particularly focuses on the role of technology as one central element of the design problem (along with customer needs and market segments). Ken Andrews' *The Concept of Corporate Strategy* (Chicago: Dow Jones Irwin, 1987) was one of the earliest formulations of the notion of strategy and strategic planning as the central responsibility of general managers. Whereas Porter (see below) provides more specific analytical tools, Andrews focuses more on the integration of strategy into the day-to-day processes of the organization.

Michael Porter's books have been very influential and are widely used. The first volume of Porter's work on strategy, *Competitive Strategy: Techniques for Analyzing Industries and Competitors* (New York: The Free Press, 1980), published over ten years ago, remains the definitive articulation of mainstream thinking on strategy design. Porter's essential insight captured in this volume is to invert the classical analyses of industrial economists, who focus on the causes and remedies of market failures. To an economist a market failure is an executive's dream—sustained and defensible competitive advantage. A generation of consultants and strategic planners began their training with this book. Although subsequent work has extended, elaborated, and periodically refuted Porter's work, his framework remains the starting point for all current discussions of competitive strategy. Porter's second volume, *Competitive*

Advantage: Creating and Sustaining Superior Performance (New York: The Free Press, 1985), documents his theories about the design and execution of strategy. This volume begins to develop arguments for the importance of execution, but his principal focus is to build a theory for strategy design.

Michael Goold and J. J. Quinn's *Strategic Control: Milestones for Long-Term Performance* (London: Economist, 1990) offers a good, comprehensive account of how to design and implement performance measurement systems that begin to link business strategy and the operational activities of the organization. This work includes substantial case studies of the strategic-level control practices of several U.K. and European organizations.

Russell Ackoff has taken an overall systems approach to the strategy process in his many articles and books. *Creating the Corporate Future* (New York: John Wiley & Sons, 1981) is representative of his thinking.

Peter Schwartz's *The Art of the Long View: Planning for the Future in an Uncertain World* (New York: Doubleday, 1991) is a well-written synthesis of thinking about scenarios and their role in planning. His personal commentary on how this way of doing strategy operated at Shell is particularly insightful. It should be read in conjunction with Pierre Wack's article on scenarios found in *Strategy: Seeking and Securing Competitive Advantage* (Boston: Harvard Business Review Books, 1991), edited by Cynthia Montgomery and Michael Porter. This anthology is an excellent presentation of much current academic thinking on strategy creation and implementation.

Information Management

Since this is an emergent field of interest, there are no texts comparable to the "classics" that are found in strategy or organization. However, within the past few years a number of studies that try to frame and analyze the key issues surrounding the management of information, regardless of its technology platform, have been published.

A good background reader is A. E. Cawkell's *Evolution of an Information Society* (London: ASLIB, 1987), which has a number of milestone articles on how information has been envisioned by both analytical and imaginative writers. *Inside the Business Enterprise: Historical Perspectives on the Use of Information* (Chicago: University of Chicago Press, 1991), edited by Peter Temin, has a number of interesting essays on the historical development of information usage. James R. Beniger's *The Control Revolution* (Cambridge, MA: Harvard University Press, 1986) is a masterful historical account of the development of "control" machinery and its implications.

Understanding Information: An Introduction (London: Macmillan, 1990), by Jonathan Liebenau and James Backhouse, is an interesting attempt to use the tools of linguistics and semantics to better understand how to work with information. *The Study of Information* (New York: John Wiley & Sons, 1983), by Fritz Machlup and Una Mansfield, is a comprehensive collection of essays, from academic points of view, on virtually every facet of the subject. *Information* (Newbury Park: SAGE Publications, 1991), by L. David Ritchie, is a concise survey of what information means, in its varied communications contexts.

A recent attempt to frame the puzzle of managing information is Blaise Cronin and Elisabeth Davenport's *Elements of Information Management* (Metuchen: The Scarecrow Press, Inc., 1991). Cronin has also edited two anthologies, published by ASLIB, both of which have interesting perspectives on this issue: *Information Management: From Strategies to Action*, Volumes 1 and 2 (London: ASLIB, 1986 and 1992).

Thomas Allen's *Managing the Flow of Technology* (Cambridge: The MIT Press, 1977) is an early attempt to understand information communications in R & D settings and is still well worth reading.

Infotrends: Profiting from your Information Resources (New York: John Wiley & Sons, 1986), by Donald A. Marchand and Forest W. Horton, Jr., moves beyond the Information Resources Management model in its attempt to offer a strategic role for information management. Horton also has written a book with Cornelius W. Burk, *InfoMap: A Complete Guide to Discovering Corporate Information Resources* (New York: Prentice Hall, 1988), which offers a more operational approach to the same issue.

Robert Taylor's *Value-Added Processes in Information Systems* (Norwood, NJ: Ablex Publishing Corporation, 1986) is an all-too-rare example of a well thought out, analytical discussion of how various processes can add value to information itself. This book should be better known to information professionals. *Information in the Enterprise*, subtitled, *It's More Than Technology* (Bedford: Digital Press, 1992), by Geoffrey Darnton and Sergio Giacoletto, is a recent attempt to understand a true information architecture, and was written, interestingly enough, by two executives of the Digital Equipment Corporation.

Executive Support Systems: The Emergence of Top Management Computer Use (Homewood: Business One Irwin, 1988), by John W. Rockart and David W. DeLong, is by far the best book on its subject and is really about information management throughout the enterprise. It thoroughly explicates the dilemmas of providing strategic information to top management. *The Information Mosaic* (Boston: Harvard Business School Press, 1992), by Sharon J. McKinnon and William J. Bruns, is a well-researched text on how information is obtained and used by the operational managers of 12 diverse organizations. The findings of this study give credence to our argument concerning the need for managers to be provided with much more than financial information.

Francis Aguilar's *Scanning the Business Environment* (New York: Macmillan, 1967), although 25 years old, remains one of the few well-researched studies on external information usage within firms. His conclusions concerning the nonsystematic ways in which managers acquire this information are still valid today. Another older but still valuable work is Henry Mintzberg's *Impediments to the Use of Management Information* (New York: National Association of Accountants, 1975). This short study initially spurred our thinking on many of the issues discussed in this text, and is well worth reading. Written in Mintzberg's lively style, the book is a good representation of a robust "counter-cultural" perspective on traditional information systems thinking.

Building the Information Architecture

A good starting point for understanding how to categorize and classify information and information systems is to read Robert Anthony's *Planning and Control Systems: A Framework for Analysis* (Cambridge: Harvard University Press, 1968). Anthony was the first researcher to clearly distinguish between strategic, managerial, and operational information, and his book has been very influential. Another "classic" in thinking about information and the systems that move was written by Peter Keen and Michael Scott Morton: *Decision Support Systems: An Organizational Perspective* (Reading: Addison–Wesley, 1978); this was one of the first books to systematically describe and define the concept of decision support, and it remains one of the best. Although the technological environment has advanced considerably, this book remains timely because of its emphasis on organizational issues and implementation challenges.

Henry Mintzberg's *The Nature of Managerial Work* (New York: Harper & Row, 1973) is a "classic" work that has influenced our approach. Mintzberg empirically researched what managers do, and he often focused on the role and nature of information in this particular "doing."

In the book *In the Age of the Smart Machine: The Future of Work and Power* (Oxford: Heinemann Professional Publishing, 1988) Shoshanna Zuboff presents an important study of how information technology is substantially changing the nature of work, and what opportunities (and threats) this change is bringing about. Her notion of "informating," as distinct from "automating," work can be a valuable perspective when thinking about organizational information usage. *Information Systems and Decision Processes* (Los Alamitos: IEEE Computer Society Press, 1992), edited by Edward A. Stohr and Benn R. Konsynski, is a good, up-to-date collection of pieces about the interaction of computer systems and human decision processes, a key consideration in designing any information architecture.

The works of Christopher Alexander, though not written specifically for information professionals, have had a significant influence on them and hold much relevance to the subject of information architecture. *Notes on the Synthesis of Form* (Cambridge: Harvard University Press, 1964) develops an interesting argument about how to do design that truly captures the needs of users. This book has become a classic among both architects and systems designers. *A Pattern Language: Towns, Buildings, Construction* (New York: Oxford University Press, 1977) argues that effective architecture builds on a language of "patterns" that humans have developed over thousands of years of testing, experimentation, and evolution. Creative designers combine these patterns in new ways to create new architectures. Again, this line of thinking bears dividends in organizational and information settings, just as it does in architectural ones. *The Timeless Way of Building* (New York: Oxford University Press, 1979), while ostensibly focused on physical architecture, is equally relevant to our discussion of information architecture and to issues of organizational structure and design.

R. Passini's *Wayfinding in Architecture* (New York: Van Nostrand Reinhold, 1992) argues that one of the tasks of architecture is to provide "clues" in the built environment that help people find their way from place to place. These clues are most effective when they tap into the basic cognitive capabilities of humans. Information architectures need to develop the same line of thinking as they apply to information spaces.

Laurence Prusak and James Matarazzo's *Information Management and Japanese Success* (Boston: Ernst & Young, 1991) surveys how eight large Japanese firms manage some of their information needs and resources. Finally, since we have been seriously discussing metaphors we should recommend *Metaphors We Live By* (Chicago: University of Chicago Press, 1980), by G. Lakoff and M. Johnson, which is a lively and fascinating exploration of how we live, work, and sometimes die by metaphors.

Organizations: How They Work and How They Learn

An excellent starting point for understanding organizations is *Images of Organizations* (Newbury Park: SAGE Publications, 1986), by Gareth Morgan. This volume provides an overview of organizations and organization theory that takes the interesting perspective of discussing competing theories of organization—mechanistic, bureaucratic, organic, cultural, political, etc.—as coequal perspectives rather than as competing alternatives. Morgan convincingly argues that this perspective is particularly relevant and important for those who hope to intervene in complex organizations to create desired changes. Several of Morgan's other works are also well worth examining. Charles Perrow's *Complex Organizations: A Critical Essay* (New York: Random House, 1986) also offers a comprehensive overview of the state of theory and thinking concerning organization design and structure.

James March's *Decision and Organizations* (Cambridge: Basil Blackwell, 1988) is a collection of wide-ranging and often witty articles by one of our leading thinkers on the ways that organizations work. Luckily, March has an interest in the role that information plays, and several of his articles are written with this perspective. Mike Pedler, John Burgoyne, and Tom Boydell have given us *The Learning Company: A Strategy for Gaining the Competitive Advantage* (London: McGraw–Hill, 1991), a quasi-anthology and running commentary with varied perspectives on how companies learn and act on that learning. D. A. Nadler, M. S. Gerstein, and R. B. Shaw show how the architectural metaphor can be effectively used in their book, *Organizational Architecture: Designs for Changing Organizations* (San Francisco: Jossey–Bass, 1992), which also emphasizes learning and change.

D. A. Schon's *Beyond the Stable State* (New York: W. W. Norton & Co., 1971) is one of the earliest efforts to work through the implications of an economic and organizational environment that is characterized by dynamic change rather than stability. It, too, offers insights into the roles of information, innovation, and learning for modern organizations. See also his well-known, *The Reflective Practitioner: How Professionals Think in Action* (New York: Basic Books, 1983).

Enterprise Networking: Working Together and Apart (Boston, MA: Digital Press, 1992), by R. Greiner and G. Metes, is one of the more interesting recent books on the impact of communications and network technologies on organization, because it was based on the experiences of two individuals in one of the prototypical network organizations, Digital Equipment Corporation. *The Corporation of the 1990s: IT and Organizational Transformation* (New York: Oxford University Press, 1991), edited by Michael S. Scott Morton, brings together several papers mostly by M.I.T. researchers on the impact of information technology and organizations and their work. *Technology for Teams: Enhancing Productivity in Networked Organizations* (New York: Van Nostrand Reinhold, 1992), by Susanna Opper and Henry Fersko–Weiss, is a useful introduction to the current state of technology for supporting group-level activity. It is targeted for a nontechnical audience and provides a good, organizationally oriented guide to implementation issues. *Connections* (Cambridge: The MIT Press, 1991), by Lee Sproull and Sara Kiesler, is another good analysis of this subject, and encompasses the social dimension.

Systems Thought and Action

Systems thinking is undergoing a resurgence in popularity, as evidenced by the success of several new books with a systems perspective. G. M. Weinberg's *An Introduction to General Systems Thinking* (New York: John Wiley & Sons, 1975) offers one of the better introductions to the topic, and is also particularly effective in making complex ideas very readable and understandable. *On the Design of Stable Systems* (New York: John Wiley & Sons, 1979) is a later continuation of the ideas contained in his introduction.

C. West Churchman has written two well-known volumes on systems thinking that have been quite influential for information systems planners. *The Design of Inquiring Systems* (New York: Basic Books, 1972) and *The Systems Approach* (New York: Delacourte Press, 1968) are particularly worth reading for an understanding of the philosophical underpinnings of systems thinking.

Peter Checkland's *Systems Thinking, Systems Practice* (New York: John Wiley & Sons, 1981) introduced a "soft-systems" approach which has been successful, especially in England, in the design of systems that integrate and incorporate within them the subjective view of key users of the system.

Peter Senge's *The Fifth Discipline: The Art and Practice of The Learning Organization* (New York: Doubleday, 1990) is a current, well-written text on how systems thinking, particularly the branch termed "industrial dynamics," can be an effective means for creating a learning organization.

Index